Easy
Beaded Crochet

Easy Beaded Crochet

Carol Meldrum

kp **kp books**
An imprint of F+W Publications, Inc.
888-457-2873

A QUARTO BOOK

Published in North America in 2006 by
Krause Publications
700 East State Street
Iola, WI 54990-0001

Library of Congress Catalog Card Number:
2006927363

ISBN-13: 978 0 89689 375 7
ISBN-10: 0 8968 9275 8

Conceived, designed, and produced by
Quarto Inc.
The Old Brewery
6 Blundell Street
London N7 9BH

QUAR.EBC

Project Editor Donna Gregory
Art Editor Julie Joubinaux
Designer Louise Clements
Photographer Sam Sloan
Photographer's Assistant Alan McRedie
Models Laura Caird, Claire Lithgow,
Gillian Cook, and Nikki Goodwin
Stylist Joanna Outhwaite
Illustrator Kate Simunek
Pattern Checker Christine Ticknor
Indexer Dorothy Frame
Assistant Art Director Penny Cobb

Art Director Moira Clinch
Publisher Paul Carslake

Color separation by
Universal Graphics Pte Ltd, Singapore
Printed by
SNP Leefung Printers Limited, China

Contents

continued
on next page ▶

Quick-and-easy projects

Brooch and pendant **72**

Beaded tunic **88**

Beaded throw **108**

Box crew-neck **76**

Bikini top **91**

Circular motif cushion **110**

Slash-neck vest **80**

Cap-sleeved wrap **94**

Beaded mat **112**

Halter-neck top **83**

Motifs for sweaters **98**

Floor cushion **114**

Cobweb shrug **86**

Appliqué cushion **104**

Coasters **118**

introduction

Over the past few years we have seen the interest in all aspects of crochet increase tremendously. Catwalk designers are incorporating this craft into their collections, and the influx of crochet into the high-street stores has really had an impact. Crochet is once again seen as being cool and hip. Traditional techniques and patterns are enjoying a new lease of life.

As the title of this book suggests, I have concentrated on beaded crochet. Beads are no longer just for trims and accents—we can play about and put them all over. There are no hard-and-fast rules when it comes to which beads or sequins to use: they just have to be big enough to fit on the yarn, or if they are too small, simply stitch them into place.

There is something for everybody—scarves, bags, hats, jewelry, projects for the home, as well as modern classic garments like the cap-sleeved wrap-over cardigan and the cobweb shrug. Each technique is fully explained and illustrated, providing you with everything you need to get started. All projects are written in the form of easy-to-follow patterns, with step-by-step instructions on any new skills required to complete a particular project, and clear photographs of what the finished piece will look like.

Choose from a wide range of inspired and original simple projects to spark the imagination and to give you the confidence to be creative with beads. Have fun working with a wide variety of yarns from 2-ply mohairs to super-chunky wools for fast, effective results. So pick up your hook, choose your beads, and get started!

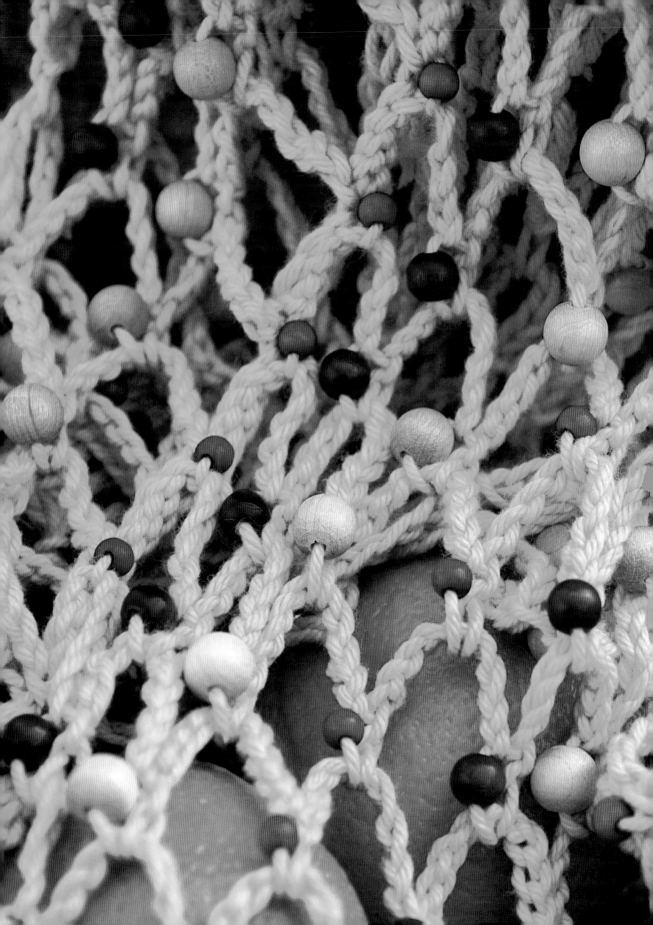

Materials, tools, & Techniques

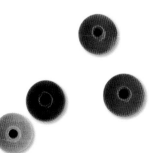

Materials

You can create a crochet fabric from almost any continuous length of fiber, but yarn is the most commonly used material. Yarns for crochet come in a wide variety of fibers, weights, colors, and price ranges, and it is important to choose the right yarn to suit your project. Although the specific yarns used to make the projects are listed on pages 122–123, you may wish to crochet a project using a different yarn. Understanding the qualities of the various types of yarn available will help you choose one that is suitable. Beads and sequins are a great way to add color to your crochet. They can give a funky feel or a touch of sophistication. Beads are available in a wide range of shapes, sizes, materials, and colors.

Yarn

Yarns are usually made by spinning together different types of fibers. The fibers may be natural materials obtained from animals or plants, for example wool or cotton, or they can be manmade fibers such as nylon or acrylic. Yarns may be made from one fiber or combine a mixture of two or three different ones in varying proportions. Several fine strands of yarn (called "plies") are often twisted together to make thicker weights of yarn. Novelty yarns, such as tweeds and other textured

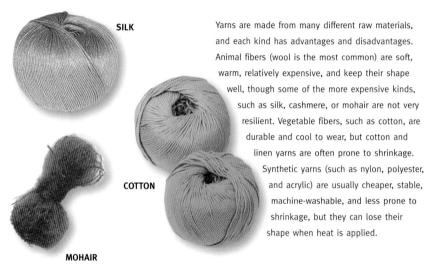

SILK

COTTON

MOHAIR

WOOL

Yarns are made from many different raw materials, and each kind has advantages and disadvantages. Animal fibers (wool is the most common) are soft, warm, relatively expensive, and keep their shape well, though some of the more expensive kinds, such as silk, cashmere, or mohair are not very resilient. Vegetable fibers, such as cotton, are durable and cool to wear, but cotton and linen yarns are often prone to shrinkage. Synthetic yarns (such as nylon, polyester, and acrylic) are usually cheaper, stable, machine-washable, and less prone to shrinkage, but they can lose their shape when heat is applied.

yarns, combine several strands of different weights and textures twisted together.

Metallic and ribbon yarns are constructed by knitting very fine yarn into tubes and giving them a rounded or flattened appearance. As a general rule, the easiest yarns to use for crochet, especially for a beginner, have a smooth surface and a medium or tight twist. These are also the best yarns to use with beads.

Yarn is sold by weight rather than by length, although the packaging of many yarns does include length per ball as well as other information. The length of yarn in the ball will vary according to thickness and fiber composition. It is usually packaged into balls, although some yarns may come in the form of hanks or skeins that need to be wound by hand into balls before you can begin to crochet.

Ball bands

The yarn you buy will have a band around it that lists lots of important information, including company brand and yarn name, weight and length of yarn, fiber content, shade and dye lot numbers, recommended needle or hook size, tension, and washing instructions.

COMPANY BRAND AND YARN NAME

WEIGHT AND LENGTH

WASHING INSTRUCTIONS

GAUGE/TENSION

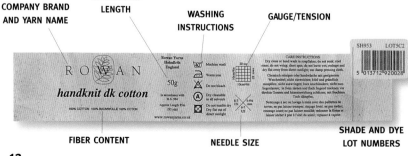

FIBER CONTENT

NEEDLE SIZE

SHADE AND DYE LOT NUMBERS

Buttons

Buttons can make or break a project, so it is worth spending a little more for an interesting button that will enhance your crochet piece. Wooden buttons are used for the projects in this book, though shell or pearlized buttons could also work. Always buy buttons after working the buttonholes to ensure a good fit.

Jewelry wire

Yarn is not the only material you can crochet with. Bracelets, necklaces, and even earrings can be made from a reel of jewelry wire. Beads can be threaded directly onto the wire without using a needle even when the wire is soft and flexible enough to crochet. Thick wires are more difficult to crochet than thin wires.

Other materials

Other materials used to make the projects in this book include cushion pads, zippers, stuffing, and jewelry fastenings. These can all be purchased from good haberdashery stores.

Yarn weights

Yarns are available in a range of thicknesses, referred to as weights, varying from very fine to very chunky. Although each weight of yarn is described by a specific name, there may actually be a lot of variation in the thicknesses when yarns are produced by different manufacturers or in different countries. There are lots of sorts of beads available nowadays; from wooden to plastic, from glass to bone, and many more besides, but it is vital to consider how well your chosen bead and yarn will go together before finalizing your choice. Use this simple checklist to guide you:

1 Will the yarn fit through the center of the bead?

2 Do the bead and yarn have similar washing requirements? High temperatures will tarnish most beads.

3 Is the bead a suitable weight for the yarn? If it is too heavy, the crocheted fabric will distort; if it is too light and small, the bead may seem lost in the yarn.

The most commonly used weights of yarn, including those used in this book, are:

sport/4-ply
• Fine yarns that are usually crocheted on hook sizes B–E (2.5–3.5 mm).

double knitting (dk)
• Slightly less than twice the thickness of sport or 4-ply yarns, usually crocheted on hook sizes E–G (3.5–4.5 mm).

worsted
• Just under twice the thickness of dk, crocheted on hook sizes H–J (5–6 mm).

aran
• Also just under twice the thickness of dk and crocheted on hook sizes H–J (5–6 mm).

bulky
• Any chunky yarn that is thicker than worsted or Aran, crocheted on hook sizes J–K (6–7 mm).

super bulky
• Really fat yarns, variously termed extra bulky, super bulky, or extra super bulky, crocheted on hook sizes L (8 mm) upward.

LINEN

VISCOSE/POLYESTER

Beads

Central to every project in this book is the use of beads, which add a glamorous touch to crocheted garments and are great for embellishing accessories. Whether worked into the fabric during crocheting or sewn on afterward, they can be used to create a range of effects—use them sparingly to create a subtle look, or liberally for a more dramatic effect.

Beads are made from a variety of materials, including plastic, bone, and wood, but the majority of the projects in this book use glass beads because of the richness of color they create.

When choosing beads, check whether they are machine washable. Also make sure that they are an appropriate size for the yarn you are using. For example, do not use large glass beads with a sport-weight yarn because they will cause the crochet to sag; similarly, avoid using very small beads with bulky-weight yarn because the beading will not stand out enough and the beads may slip through the stitches to the wrong side of the fabric, especially if it is not knitted very tightly.

Always make sure that the hole in the center of the bead is big enough to pass a doubled end of yarn through. When knitting with two ends of yarn at the same time, thread the beads onto the finer yarn, hold the ends of both yarns together, and work as normal.

Seed beads

These small, round glass beads are ideal for embellishing knitted fabrics. They can be sewn onto the finished item, but are also very easy to incorporate into the fabric during knitting. Seed beads are available in a wide variety of sizes and in many different finishes. Some are made with colored glass, while others are transparent and lined with color, which means that the central hole has been painted with color. Seed beads are commonly sold by gram weight.

Decorative beads

As well as using seed beads, the projects in this book feature a variety of other decorative beads. Some of the more common types of bead are bugles (long, thin, cylinder-shaped beads), cubes, triangles, daggers, and Magatamas (teardrop). A quick browse through a bead store, catalog, or website will also reveal beads in the shape of leaves, flowers, faces, fish, bicones, crystals, stars... The list goes on and on, and all of these beads are beautiful. When choosing beads for crochet projects, remember to check that the hole is an appropriate size for your yarn, and that the bead itself is quite smooth (inside and out), or it will damage your finished article. If used for garments (as opposed to jewelry or accessories), odd-shaped beads may be uncomfortable for the wearer.

Glass beads are available in a wide range of colors and sizes.

There are lots of different kinds of decorated beads, such as these Kenyan ceramic beads.

TIP: BUYING BEADS

Even if a pattern or book project states exactly how many beads are required, it is always best to buy more than specified if possible. This is particularly important with small seed beads. You may have to discard some beads as you work, perhaps because they are sharp-edged or misshapen, or you may break or lose some. Beads are made and dyed in batches, so if you have to buy more beads to finish a piece, you may well find that the new beads vary in color from those in the rest of the project. It may also take some time before your bead stockist has more supplies, or a color may occasionally be discontinued.

Keep beads in shallow containers while you are working with them.

There is a huge array of compartmentalized boxes for storing your beads, and these are invaluable both for storing your beads in, and for keeping your colors seprate when working on a project.

Choosing beads

The sheer variety of colors, sizes, and finishes of beads can be bewildering. Here is a handy guide to help you to decide which bead you should choose for your project.

Sizing

Beads come in a variety of sizes. Glass seed beads, which are perfect for incorporating into crochet designs, are most often sold in size 11/0, though be aware that sizes may vary slightly between manufacturers. Using beads of different sizes within one piece can cause the gauge to vary, so it is better to keep the beads all the same size.

Colors

Made from glass, seed beads come in a stunning range of colors, finishes, and sizes. You can find a color to suit every design, and they are more than a little addictive!

The beads themselves can be:

Transparent—made of clear glass so you can see right through the bead.

Translucent—the glass is slightly milky, so light can still pass through it.

Opaque—the glass is a solid color, and light cannot pass through it.

Silver-lined—the hole at the center of the bead has a mirror-like lining, making the bead sparkle.

Color-lined—the hole through the center of the bead is lined with a different color.

Satin—the glass is striated, giving an effect like the mineral tiger's-eye, or satin fabric.

Finishes

As well as color, there can also be a finish applied to the surface of the bead, such as:

AB—*Aurora borealis*. A clear rainbow finish over the bead, similar to that seen on oil in water.

Iris—an iridescent finish applied to an opaque glass bead, giving it a metallic look.

Luster—a shiny finish. This can be clear, colored, or metallic—for example, gold luster beads which have a lovely warm glow. An opaque lustered bead is called "pearl" and a translucent lustered bead is called "ceylon."

Matt—the glass is etched, giving a soft, frosted finish.

Metallic/galvanized—a metal finish or coating applied to the bead. Although some of these can last well, this finish can wear off with handling.

Painted/dyed—some beads are painted or dyed. Although these beads are beautiful, paint can wear off when the beads are handled or fade in sunlight.

Pearls can be used to crochet with, and will add a sophisticated touch to any garment.

Wooden beads can be stained, painted, varnished, or natural.

Some of these Czech matt glass beads have a special *Aurora Borealis* (AB) finish.

Tools

Very little equipment is needed for crochet—all you really require is a hook, although items such as pins and scissors are useful and relatively inexpensive. The tools mentioned here are the basics; others can be bought as you go along.

ALUMINUM AND RESIN HOOKS

Hooks

Crochet hooks are available in a wide range of sizes, shapes, and materials. The most common sorts of hooks used for working with the types of yarns covered in this book are made from aluminum or plastic. Small sizes of steel hooks are also made for working crochet with very fine cotton yarns. (This type of fine yarn is known as crochet thread.) Some brands of aluminum and steel hooks have plastic handles to give a better grip (often called "soft touch" handles) and make the work easier on the fingers. Handmade wooden and horn hooks are also available, many featuring decorative handles. Bamboo hooks are great to work with because they are made from a natural material and have a very smooth finish.

Crochet hooks come in a range of sizes, from very fine to very thick. Finer yarns usually require a smaller hook, thicker yarns a larger hook. There appears to be no standardization of hook sizing between manufacturers. The points and throats of different brands of hooks often vary in shape, which affects the size of stitch they produce.

Hook sizes are quoted differently in Europe and the US, and some brands of hooks are labeled with more than one type of numbering. The hook sizes quoted in pattern instructions are a useful guide, but you may find that you need to use smaller or larger hook sizes, depending on the brand, to achieve the correct gauge for the pattern (see page 31).

Choosing a hook is largely a matter of personal preference and will depend on various factors such as hand size, finger length, weight of hook, and whether you like the feel of aluminum or plastic in your hand. The most important things to consider when choosing a hook is how it feels in your hand and the ease with which it works with your yarn. When you have found your perfect brand of hook, it is useful to buy a range of several different sizes. Store your hooks in a clean container—you can buy a fabric roll with loops to secure the hooks, or use a zippered purse such as a cosmetic bag.

POINT — THROAT — THUMB REST — SHANK

Comparative crochet hook sizes (from smallest to largest)					
US	UK	METRIC (MM)	US	UK	METRIC (MM)
14	6	0.60		14	2.00
13	5½			13	
12	5	0.75	B	12	2.50
11	4½		C	11	3.00
10	4	1.00	D	10	
9	3½		E	9	3.50
8	3	1.25	F	8	4.00
7	2½	1.50	G	7	4.50
6	2	1.75	H	6	5.00
5	1½		I	5	5.50
4	1	2.00	J	4	6.00
3	1/0		K	2	7.00
2	2/0	2.50	L	1	8.00
1	3/0	3.00	N	0	9.00
0			P	00	10.0000 3.50

Markers

Split rings or shaped loops made from brightly colored plastic can be slipped onto your crochet to mark a place on a pattern, to indicate the beginning row of a repeat, and to help with counting the stitches on the foundation chain.

MARKERS

Sewing needles

Tapestry needles have blunt points and long eyes and are normally used for counted thread embroidery. They come in a range of sizes and are used for weaving in yarn ends and for sewing pieces of crochet together. Very large blunt-pointed needles are often labeled as "yarn needles." You may also need a selection of sewing needles with sharp points for applying crochet edging, working embroidery stitches, and so on.

SEWING NEEDLES

Tape measure

Choose one that shows both inches and centimeters on the same side and replace it when it becomes worn or frayed because this means it will probably have stretched and become inaccurate. A 12-in. (30-cm) metal or plastic ruler is also useful for measuring gauge swatches.

TAPE MEASURE

Pins

Glass-headed rustproof pins are the best type to use for blocking (see pages 32–33). Plastic-headed or pearl-headed pins can be used for pinning crochet and for cold-water blocking, but do not use this type for warm-steam blocking because the heat of the iron will melt the plastic heads. Quilters' long pins with fancy heads are useful when pinning pieces of crochet together because the heads are easy to see and will not slip through the crochet fabric.

Row counter

A knitter's row counter will help you keep track of the number of rows you have worked, or you may prefer to use a notebook and pencil.

ROW COUNTER

GLASS-HEADED PINS

QUILTERS' PINS

SHARP SCISSORS

Notebook

Keep a small notebook handy to record where you are in the pattern or any changes you have made.

Sharp scissors

Choose a small, pointed pair to cut yarn and trim off yarn ends.

Sewing thread

This is used to thread the beads onto the yarn.

SEWING THREAD

Getting started

The first step when beginning to crochet is to create a foundation chain of loops. It is also important to hold the hook and yarn correctly. There are numerous ways of doing this, but the best method is the one that feels most comfortable to you.

Making a slip knot

All crochet is made up from one loop on the hook at any time. The first working loop begins as a slip knot. The first loop does not count as a stitch.

1

1 Take the short end of the yarn in one hand and wrap it around the forefinger on your other hand.

2

2 Slip the loop off your forefinger and push a loop of the short end of the yarn through the loop from your forefinger.

3

3 Insert the hook into this second loop. Gently pull the short end of the yarn to tighten the loop around the hook and complete the slip knot.

Holding the hook

There are a few different methods of holding the hook and yarn. There is no right or wrong way. The most important thing is to use the method that you prefer and the type of hook that you find most comfortable.

Pen hold

Hold the hook as if it were a pen, with the tips of your thumb and forefinger over the flat section or middle of the hook.

Knife hold

Hold the hook as if it were a knife, almost grasping the flat section or middle of the hook between your thumb and forefinger.

Holding the yarn

It is important to wrap the yarn around your fingers to control the supply of yarn and to keep the gauge even. You can hold the yarn in several ways, but again it is best to use the method that feels the most comfortable.

1

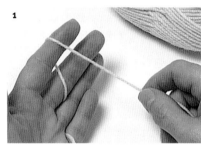

1 Loop the short end of the yarn over your forefinger, with the yarn coming from the ball under the next finger. Grip the length of yarn coming from the ball gently with your third and little fingers.

2

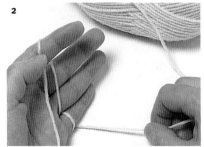

2 Alternatively, loop the short end of the yarn over your forefinger, with the yarn coming from the ball under your next two fingers and then wrapped around the little finger.

Foundation chains

From the slip knot, you can now create a foundation chain (this is similar to casting on in knitting). This chain determines the width of the work.

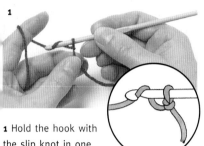

1 Hold the hook with the slip knot in one hand. With your other hand, grip the shorter piece of yarn just under the slip knot with your thumb and middle finger, and hold the longer piece of yarn over the forefinger. To create the first chain stitch, use your forefinger to wrap the yarn over the hook (known as "yarn over").

2 Draw the wrapped yarn toward you and through the slip knot already on the hook to make a new loop and complete the chain stitch.

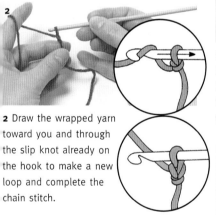

3 Repeat this process, remembering to move your thumb and middle finger up the chain as it lengthens. When counting the chain stitches, each V-shaped loop on the front of the chain counts as one, except the one on the hook, which is known as a working stitch.

Beaded foundation chain

Incorporating beads into the foundation chain is very easy to do.

1 Make a slip knot in the usual way, then bring a bead up to the top of the yarn, place the bead under the hook, and wrap the yarn over the hook.

2 Pull the yarn through the loop, leaving the bead at the front of the work, lying on the chain. Continue in this way for each beaded chain stitch required in the pattern.

TIP: COUNTING STITCHES

The front of the chain looks like a series of V shapes, while the back of the chain forms a distinctive "bump" of yarn behind each V shape. When counting chain stitches, count each V shape on the front of the chain as one chain stitch, except for the chain stitch on the hook, which is not counted. You may find it easier to turn the chain over and count the "bumps" on the back of the chain.

Adding beads and sequins

It is easy to incorporate beads and sequins into crochet fabrics. Any type of beads and sequins can be used, provided that the central hole is large enough for the yarn to pass through. See pages 14–15 for ideas.

1 Thread a sewing needle with a short length of sewing cotton and knot the ends. Pass the yarn through the loop made. Slide each bead or sequin onto the needle, then down the sewing cotton and onto the yarn. Pull the yarn through and continue threading on beads or sequins in this way.

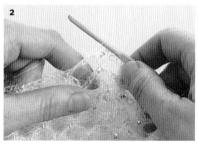

2 When indicated in the pattern, push a bead or sequin up the yarn to sit just below the crochet hook. Work the next stitch as instructed—in this case, single crochet—leaving the bead or sequin at the front of the work.

Working into the foundation chain

The first row of stitches is worked into the foundation chain. There are two ways of doing this, with the first method being easiest for the beginner.

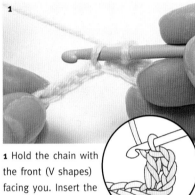

1 Hold the chain with the front (V shapes) facing you. Insert the hook into the top loop of each chain stitch. This gives a loose edge to a piece of crochet.

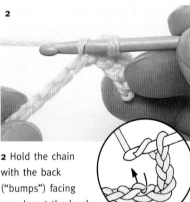

2 Hold the chain with the back ("bumps") facing you. Insert the hook into the "bump" at the back of each chain stitch. This makes a stronger, neater edge.

Turning chains

When working crochet, you need to work a specific number of extra chain stitches at the beginning of a row or round. These stitches are called a turning chain when worked at the beginning of a straight row and a starting chain when worked at the beginning of a round. What they do is bring the hook up to the correct height for the next stitch to be worked, so the longer the stitch, the longer the turning chain that is necessary.

The patterns in this book specify how many chain stitches need to be worked at the beginning of a row or round. The list below shows the standard number of chain stitches needed to make a turn for each type of basic crochet stitch, but a pattern may vary from this in order to produce a specific effect. If you have a tendency to work chain stitches very tightly, you may need to work an extra chain stitch in order to keep the edges of your work from becoming too tight.

Number of turning chain stitches

- Single crochet = 1 turning chain
- Extended single crochet = 2 turning chains
- Half double crochet = 2 turning chains
- Double crochet = 3 turning chains
- Treble crochet = 4 turning chains

> **TIP: WORKING WITH TURNING CHAINS**
> The turning or starting chain is counted as the first stitch of the row except when working single crochet, when the turning chain is ignored. At the end of the row or round, the final stitch is usually worked into the turning or starting chain of the previous row or round.

Longer stitches, such as the double crochet used to make this tunic (pages 88–90), require more turning chains than short stitches such as single crochet.

Basic stitches

Various stitches can be worked onto the foundation chain to form a crochet fabric. Each stitch gives a different texture and varies in depth.

TIP: NUMBER OF CHAINS

This diagram shows the number of chains from the hook. Different crochet stitches are worked a different number of chains from the hook. For example, single crochet is usually worked through the second chain from the hook, while double crochet is worked through the fourth chain from the hook.

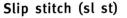

Single crochet (sc)

This is the easiest of crochet fabrics to create, producing a compact fabric that is still flexible.

1 Work the foundation chain plus one extra chain stitch (this is the turning chain). Insert the hook from front to back through the second chain from the hook. Wrap the yarn over the hook and draw the yarn through the chain toward you, leaving two loops on the hook.

2

2 Wrap the yarn over the hook again and draw it through both loops on the hook. This leaves one loop on the hook and completes the stitch.

3

3 Continue in this way along the row, working one single crochet stitch into each chain stitch.

4

4 At the end of the row, turn, and work one chain for the turning chain. When working double crochet back along the row, insert the hook from front to back under both loops of the single crochet stitches of the previous row.

5

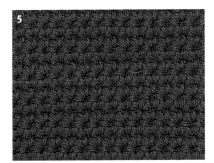

5 Fabric composed entirely of single crochet stitches is compact but flexible.

Slip stitch (sl st)

This is commonly used to join ends of work together to form a ring or to work across the top of other stitches invisibly. Insert the hook from front to back into the last chain just worked. Wrap the yarn over the hook, then draw the yarn toward you through both the chain and the loop on the hook.

Extended single crochet (exsc)

As its name suggests, this stitch is slightly longer than a single crochet stitch.

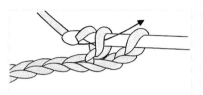

1 Work the foundation chain plus two extra chain stitches (this is the turning chain). Insert the hook from front to back through the third chain from the hook. Wrap the yarn over the hook and draw the yarn through the chain toward you, leaving two loops on the hook.

2 Wrap the yarn over the hook again and draw it through the first loop on the hook, again leaving two loops on the hook.

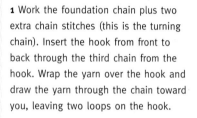

3 Wrap the yarn over the hook again and draw it through both loops on the hook.

4 This leaves one loop on the hook and completes the stitch. Continue in this way along the row, working one extended single crochet into each chain stitch.

At the end of the row, turn and work two chains for the turning chain. When working extended single crochet back along the row, insert the hook from front to back under both loops of the extended single crochet stitches of the previous row.

Double crochet (dc)

Double crochet is a longer stitch than single crochet, creating a more open and flexible fabric. The stitch is similar, except that you wrap the yarn over the hook before working into the fabric.

1 Work the foundation chain plus three extra chain stitches (this is the turning chain). Wrap the yarn over the hook, then insert the hook from front to back into the fourth chain from the hook.

2 Wrap yarn over the hook again and draw the yarn through the chain toward you, leaving three loops on the hook.

3 Wrap the yarn over the hook again and draw it through the first two loops, leaving two loops on the hook.

4 Wrap the yarn over the hook again and draw it through the last two loops.

5 This leaves one loop on the hook and completes the stitch. Continue in this way along the row, working one double crochet into each chain stitch.

6 At the end of the row, turn and work three chains for the turning chain. When working double crochet back along the row, skip the first double crochet stitch at the beginning of the row and insert the hook from front to back through both loops of each remaining double crochet stitches of the previous row. At the end of the row, work the last stitch into the top of the turning chain.

7 Fabric composed entirely of double crochet stitches is still firm, like single crochet fabric, but slightly more open and flexible.

Half double crochet (hdc)

This stitch is slightly shorter than the double crochet stitch.

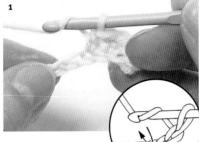

1 Work the foundation chain plus two extra chain stitches (this is the turning chain). Wrap the yarn over the hook, then insert the hook from front to back into the third chain from the hook.

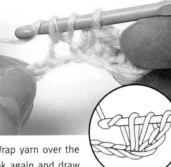

2 Wrap yarn over the hook again and draw the yarn through the chain toward you, leaving three loops on the hook. Wrap the yarn over the hook again and draw it through all three loops. This leaves one loop on the hook and completes the stitch.

3 Continue in this way along the row, working one half double crochet into each chain stitch. At the end of the row, turn and work two chains for the turning chain.

4 When working half double crochet back along the row, skip the first half double crochet stitch at the beginning of the row, then insert the hook from front to back under both loops of each remaining half double crochet stitch of the previous row.

5 At the end of the row, work the last stitch into the top of the turning chain.

6 Fabric composed entirely of half double crochet stitches is firm and flexible, but not as compact as single crochet or double crochet fabric.

Treble crochet (tr)

This stitch is slightly longer than the double crochet stitch.

1 Work the foundation chain plus four extra chain stitches (this is the turning chain). Wrap the yarn over the hook twice, then insert the hook from front to back into the fifth chain from the hook. Wrap the yarn over the hook again and draw the yarn through the chain toward you, leaving four loops on the hook.

2 Wrap the yarn over the hook again and draw it through the first two loops, leaving three loops on the hook.

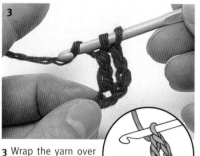

3 Wrap the yarn over the hook again and draw it through the first two loops, leaving two loops on the hook. Wrap the yarn over the hook again and draw it under the last two loops. This leaves one loop on the hook and completes the stitch.

4 Continue in this way along the row, working one treble crochet into each chain stitch. At the end of the row, turn and work four chains for the turning chain. When working treble crochet back along the row, skip the first treble crochet stitch at the beginning of the row, then insert the hook from front to back through both loops of the remaining treble crochet stitches of the previous row. At the end of the row, work the last stitch into the top of the turning chain.

5 Fabric composed entirely of treble crochet stitches is open and very flexible.

Joining new yarn or color

It is best to join a new yarn at the end of a row, but you can join a new yarn anywhere in a row if you need to. Leave the last stage of the final stitch incomplete, loop the new yarn over the hook, and use it to complete the stitch. Work the next row in the new yarn or color. When changing color in the middle of a row, begin the stitch in the usual way, wrap the new yarn over the hook, draw the new yarn through the stitch toward you, and then work the stitch.

Working into front and back of stitches

It is usual to work crochet stitches under both loops of the stitches made on the previous row. However, sometimes a pattern will instruct you to work under just one loop, either the back or the front, in which case the remaining loop becomes a horizontal bar.

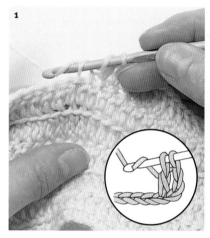

1 To work into the front of a row of stitches, insert the hook under only the front loops of the stitches on the previous row.

2 To work into the back of a row of stitches, insert the hook under only the back loops of the stitches on the previous row. Working into the back of the stitch creates a strongly ridged fabric.

Working in rounds

Some circular pieces of crochet require that you work in rounds rather than rows. The basic stitch techniques are the same, but you work around the work rather than back and forth.

Making a ring

To start, you have to make a ring by joining a small length of chain with a slip stitch. The chain is usually between 4 and 6 stitches, depending on the thickness of yarn being used.

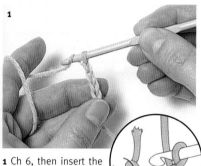

1 Ch 6, then insert the hook from front to back through the first chain made.

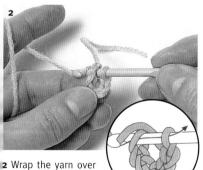

2 Wrap the yarn over the hook and draw it toward you through the chain and loop on the hook, as if working a slip stitch (see page 21).

3 Gently tighten the first stitch by pulling the loose yarn end. You have now created a ring of chains.

Working into the ring

The foundation ring is the center of your circular crochet and where you will work into on the next round.

1 Depending on the stitch you will be using, make the appropriate length of starting chain (see page 20).

TIP: MARKING ROUNDS

Place a marker at the beginning of the round. This will help to show where the round stops and starts because sometimes it can be tricky to tell. Simply pull the marker out at the end of each round and reposition it for the next.

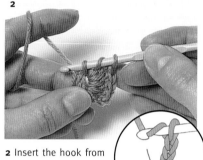

2 Insert the hook from front to back into the center of the ring (not into the chain) for each stitch and work the number of stitches specified in the pattern. Remember when working in rounds that the right side is always facing you.

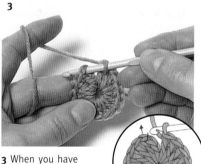

3 When you have worked around the full circle, finish off the round by working a slip stitch into the top of the starting chain worked at the beginning of the round.

Shaping techniques

Shaping your crochet is done by increasing or decreasing stitches along a row. When adding or subtracting stitches at intervals along a row, this is called internal increase or decrease. When stitches are added or subtracted at the beginning or end of a row, this is called external increase or decrease. Each method creates a different effect.

Internal increases

This is the simplest method of adding stitches at intervals along a row.

1 Work to the point where you want to increase, then work two or more stitches into one stitch on the previous row.

2 This method is often used one stitch in from the edge at the beginning and end of a row to shape garment edges neatly. At the beginning of the row, work the first stitch and then work the increase as described in step 1.

3 At the end of the row, work to the last two stitches, work the increase in the next to last stitch as described in step 1, and then work the last stitch.

External increases

This method can be used to increase several stitches at one time. You will need to add extra foundation chains at the beginning or end of a row.

1 To add stitches at the beginning of a row, work the required number of extra chains at the end of the previous row and remember to add the turning chains.

2 On the next row, work the extra stitches along the chain and then continue along the row.

3 To add stitches at the end of a row, leave the last few stitches of the row unworked. Remove the hook and join a length of yarn to the last stitch of the row and work the required number of extra foundation chains. Fasten off the yarn.

4 Place the hook back into the row, complete the row, and then continue working the extra stitches across the chain.

Internal decreases

As with the internal increases, if you are decreasing stitches in order to create a neat edge when shaping, always work the decrease one stitch in from the edge.

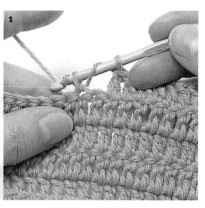

1 The easiest way to decrease stitches across a row is simply to skip one stitch of the previous row.

2 Alternatively, two stitches can be worked together. Start working the first stitch of the decrease but do not complete it; instead, leave two loops on the hook. Insert the hook into the next stitch and work another incomplete stitch so that you have three loops on the hook. Wrap the yarn over the hook and draw it through all three loops on the hook.

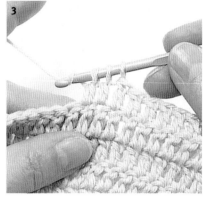

3 The same method can also be used for decreasing more than two stitches. In this example, three stitches are decreased by working them together.

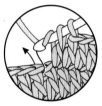

External decreases

This method is best used if you want to decrease several stitches at one time.

1 To decrease at the beginning of a row, work a slip stitch (see page 21) into each of the stitches that you want to decrease, then work the turning chains and continue along the row.

2 To decrease at the end of a row, leave the stitches to be decreased unworked. Work the turning chains, then turn and work along the next row.

Shaping techniques, used to make projects such as this ear-flap hat (pages 68–69), are easy to learn.

Lace work

Lace motifs are light, pretty, and delicate to look at when worked in light-weight yarns, and are perfect for making shawls, wraps, and stoles. It is usual to join several motifs to make a strip, then add further motifs along one long edge of the strip until you have two strips joined together. Keep adding motifs until you have joined the required number of strips together.

Chain spaces

Long strands of chain stitches, described as chain spaces, chain loops, or chain arches, are an integral part of lace motif patterns. They are sometimes used as a foundation for stitches worked in the following round, or they may form a visible part of the design.

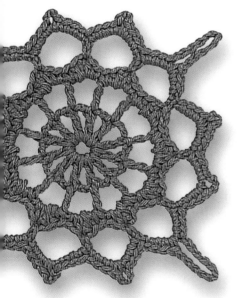

Lace motifs are very effective when joined together to make garments such as the cobweb shrug (pages 86–87).

Changing the hook position

Working in slip stitch (see page 21) across one or more stitches is a useful way of changing the position of the yarn and hook on a round. Pattern directions may refer to this technique as "slip stitch across" or "slip stitch into." Here, slip stitches are being worked into the edge of a petal in order to move the hook and yarn from the valley between two petals to the tip of one petal, ready to work the next sequence of stitches.

1 Work chain spaces as evenly as possible, anchoring them by working a slip stitch or single crochet into the previous round.

2 When a chain space is worked as a foundation on one row, stitches are worked over the chains on the following row. To do this, simply insert the hook into the space below the strand of chain stitches to work each stitch, not directly into individual chain stitches.

Joining lace motifs

Lace motifs are usually joined together on the final pattern round
as you work, eliminating the need for sewing.

1

1 Complete the first motif. Work the
second motif up to the last round, then
work the first side of the last round,
ending at the specified point where the
first join will be made, in this case halfway
along a chain space at the corner of the
motif.

2

2 Place the first and second motifs' wrong
sides together, ready to work the next
side of the second motif. Join the chain
spaces with a single crochet stitch, then
complete the chain space on the second
motif. Continue along the same side of
the second motif, joining chain spaces
together with single crochet stitches.

3

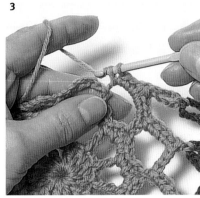

3 After all the chain spaces along one side
are joined, complete the second motif in
the usual way. Work additional motifs in
the same way, joining the required number
together to make a strip.

4

4 Work the first motif of the second strip,
stopping when you have reached the
joining point. Place against the side of
the top motif in the first strip (wrong
sides together) and join the chain spaces
as before. When you reach the point where
three corner chain spaces meet, work the
single crochet into the stitch joining the
two existing motifs.

5

5 Work the second motif of the second
strip, stopping when you have reached the
joining point. Place against the side of the
first motif in the second strip (wrong sides
together) and join the chain spaces as
before. When you reach the point where
all four corner chain spaces meet, work
the single crochet into the stitch joining
the first two motifs.

6

6 Now join the next side of the motif to
the adjacent side of the first strip, working
single crochet stitches into chain spaces as
before. Complete the remaining sides
of the motif. Continue working in the same
way until you have made and joined the
required number of motifs.

Understanding patterns

Crochet pattern instructions are laid out in a logical sequence, although at first sight the terminology can look complicated. The most important thing is to check that you start off with the correct number of stitches in the foundation row or ring, and then work through the instructions row by row exactly as stated. All of the patterns in this book use written instructions rather than charts.

This pashmina (pages 44–45) may look complex, but the pattern is short and easy to learn.

Crochet abbreviations

The abbreviations used in this book are:

bch—beaded chain
bsc—beaded single crochet
C2—yo twice, draw loop through stitch just worked, (yo, draw loop through first 2 loops on hook) twice, skip 2 stitches, yo twice, draw loop through next stitch, (yo, draw loop through first 2 loops on hook) twice, yo, draw loop through remaining 3 loops on hook
ch—chain
dc—double crochet
dec—decrease
exsc—extended single crochet
hdc—half double crochet
inc—increase
sc—single crochet
sl st—slip stitch
st(s)—stitch(es)
tr—treble or triple crochet
yo—yarn over

Essential information

All patterns provide a list containing the size of the finished item, the materials and hook size required, the gauge of the piece, and the abbreviations used in the instructions. Although many abbreviations are standardized, such as ch for chain and st for stitch, some of them vary, so always read the abbreviations before you start crocheting.

Repeats

When following the pattern instructions, you will find that some of them appear within curved parentheses and some are marked with an asterisk. Instructions that appear within parentheses are to be repeated. For example, (1 dc into next 3 sts, ch 2) 4 times means that you work the 3 double crochet stitches and the 2 chains in the sequence stated four times in all. Asterisks (*) indicate the point to which you should return when you reach the phrase "repeat from *." They may also mark whole sets of instructions that are to be repeated. For example, "repeat from * to **" means repeat the instructions between the single and double asterisks.

You may also find asterisks used in instructions that tell you how to work any stitches remaining after the last complete repeat of a stitch sequence is worked. For example, repeat from *, ending with 1 sc into each of last 2 sts, turn, means that you have two stitches left at the end of

TIP: TAKE NOTES

Each stitch pattern worked in rows is written using a specific number of pattern rows and the sequence is repeated until the crochet is the correct length. When working a complicated stitch pattern, always make a note of exactly which row you are working.

the row after working the last repeat. In this case, work one single crochet into each of the last two stitches before turning to begin the next row.

Additional information

You may find a number enclosed in parentheses at the end of a row or round. This indicates the total number of stitches to be worked in that particular row or round. For example, (12 spaced dc) at the end of a round means that you have to work 12 double crochet stitches in the round, each one spaced by the number of chains stated in the instructions.

Gauge/Tension

The term "gauge" (or "tension") refers to the number of stitches and rows contained in a given width and length of crochet fabric, usually 4 in. (10 cm) square. You will find that everybody has their own personal gauge when working a crochet fabric. It varies from person to person, even when the same yarn and hook size are used. Crochet patterns are written using a specific gauge in mind and, if your gauge differs from the one given, the finished piece could come out either too big or too small. That is why it is important to check your gauge before starting a pattern.

Making a test swatch

Using the recommended hook size and yarn, make a crochet piece approx 6–8 in. (15–20 cm) square, taking into account the number of stitches and rows in the stitch pattern. Fasten off and then block the sample (see pages 32–33). It is vital to work the gauge sample in the exact pattern you will use for the main piece.

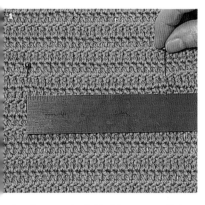

1 Lay the sample right side up on a flat surface. Using a ruler or tape measure, measure 4 in. (10 cm) horizontally across a row of stitches. Insert pins exactly 4 in. (10 cm) apart and count the number of stitches (including partial stitches) between the pins.

2 Turn the fabric on its side. Using a ruler or tape measure, measure 4 in. (10 cm) horizontally across the rows. Insert pins exactly 4 in. (10 cm) apart and count the number of rows (including partial rows) between the pins.

3 When working a stitch pattern, the gauge may be quoted as a multiple of the pattern repeat rather than a number of stitches and rows. Work the gauge sample in pattern, but count the number of pattern repeats between the pins.

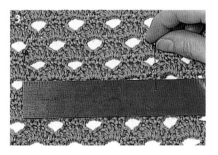

Adjusting your gauge

If the number of stitches, rows, or pattern repeats to 4 in. (10 cm) match the pattern, you can get started. If you have too many stitches or rows or a smaller pattern repeat, your crochet is too tight—use a larger hook. If you have too few stitches or rows or a larger pattern repeat, your crochet is too loose—use a smaller hook. Block and measure the new gauge sample as before. Repeat this process until your gauge matches that given in the pattern.

TIP: HOOKS AND YARNS
Hooks and yarns from different manufacturers or in different materials can vary in size even if they are all branded the same. Always work a sample swatch to check that the pattern works for your materials.

How beads affect gauge

Adding beads may slacken your gauge slightly at the beginning if you have not used this technique before, as you can be so busy concentrating on placing the bead correctly that you forget about the gauge!

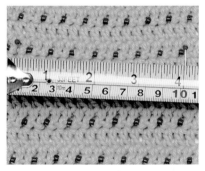

Using a bead that is bigger than your stitch will also affect your gauge. Be prepared to experiment before finalizing your design if you are straying from a pattern. Until you are used to crocheting with beads, stick to the beads, yarn, and tension as set out in the pattern.

Finishing techniques

*A beautifully crocheted garment can easily be ruined by careless sewing up.
Use a tapestry needle and a length of the yarn used to crochet the project, and
select the method most suitable for the finished effect you want to achieve. Most
crocheted fabrics need to be blocked before they are stitched together.*

Fastening off

When your work is completed, you need to fasten off the yarn to stop
it from unraveling. This is called fastening off or binding off.

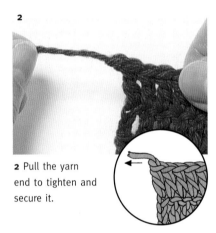

1 Cut the yarn,
leaving a length
of about 4–6 in.
(10–15 cm). Draw the
loose end through the last
loop on the hook.

2 Pull the yarn
end to tighten and
secure it.

Weaving in ends

After fastening off the yarn, you need to weave in all the loose ends.
Thread the end through a blunt-ended needle with a large eye. Weave all the loose
ends into the work, running them through the stitches nearest to the yarn end.

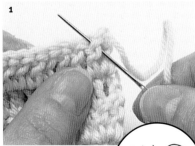

1 At the top edge of
the work, weave the
end through several
stitches on the wrong
side. Cut off the excess yarn.

2 At the lower edge
of the work, weave the
end through several
stitches on the wrong
side. Cut off the excess yarn.

Blocking and pressing

When all the ends are woven in and
before you start sewing the pieces
together, you need to block and press
them to the correct size and shape. To
block crochet, pin the pieces onto a
padded surface. Depending on the size
of the piece you want to block, a variety
of things can be used—ironing board, large
pillow, a board covered with one or two
layers of quilter's batting, or even the floor.
Cover the padded surface with a check
pattern cotton fabric. This will not only
help when pinning straight edges, but also
will withstand the heat of an iron. When
choosing how to press the crochet pieces,
refer to the information given on the ball
band of the yarn.

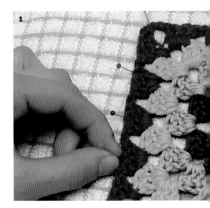

1 Pin the pieces right side downward onto
a padded surface using rustless glass-
headed pins (plastic may melt) inserted
at right angles to the edge of the crochet.
Ease the crochet piece into shape, making
sure that the stitches and rows are
straight. Measure to check that each
pinned out piece matches the finished
size stated in the pattern.

2 For natural fibers such as wool or cotton, set the iron on a steam setting. Hold the iron approximately 1 in. (2.5 cm) above the fabric and allow the steam to penetrate for several seconds. Work in sections and avoid the iron touching the work. Lay flat and allow to dry before removing the pins.

3 Pin crochet pieces made from synthetic fibers as described in step 1. Do not use a dry or a steam iron. When heat is applied to synthetics, they lose their luster and go very limp; in the worst cases you can melt the crochet and ruin your iron. When pinned out, spray the crochet fabric lightly with cold water until evenly moist but not soaked through. Lay flat and allow to dry before taking out the pins.

Seams

There are several methods for joining pieces of crochet together, including sewing the seams using a sewing needle or working a row of crochet stitches through the edges of the pieces using a crochet hook. It is really a matter of personal preference unless a pattern specifies a particular method. Use the one you are most comfortable with and that gives you the best finish. Seams are usually worked using the same yarn used for the main pieces, but a contrasting color yarn can be used to make a decorative statement. A contrasting color is used in these examples for clarity.

Overcast seam

Pieces of crochet can be joined by overcasting the seam. The overcasting stitches can be worked through just the back of the crochet loops or the whole loops. Place the pieces to be joined side-by side on a flat surface with right sides facing up and edges together. Thread a large blunt-ended sewing needle with yarn.

1 Working from right to left, overcast the seam by inserting the needle into the back loop of corresponding stitches. For extra strength, you can work two stitches into the end loops.

2 Continue overcasting the seam, making sure you join only the back loops of the edges together, until you reach the end of the seam. Secure the yarn carefully at the beginning and end of the stitching.

3 Alternatively, overcast the two pieces together by inserting the needle through the whole loops of corresponding stitches. This gives a less neat join than sewing through just the back of the loops.

Backstitch seam

This creates a strong but non-elastic seam and is suitable where firmness is required and for light-weight yarns. With right sides facing each other, pin together the pieces to be joined. Insert the pins at right-angles to the edge evenly across the fabric. Thread a large blunt-ended sewing needle with yarn.

Single crochet seam

Place the pieces to be joined right sides together. Using a crochet hook and working from right to left, work a row of single crochet stitches through both layers (see page 21).

2 Work in backstitch from right to left along the whole seam, making sure that you stay close to the edge and go through both pieces of fabric. Secure the end with a couple of overlapping stitches.

1 Secure the end of the seam and yarn by taking the needle twice around the outer edges of the fabric, from back to front. Take the yarn around the outside edge once more, but this time insert the needle through the work from back to front no more than ½ in. (1.3 cm) from where the yarn last came out. Insert the needle from front to back at the point where the first stitch began, then bring the needle back through to the front, the same distance along the edge as before.

Slip stitch seam

Joining pieces by slip stitching them together with a crochet hook makes a firm seam with an attractive ridge on the right side. Place the pieces wrong sides together and work a row of slip stitch through both layers (see page 21).

Woven seam

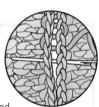

Place the pieces to be joined side by side on a flat surface, with wrong sides facing up and edges together. Thread a large blunt-ended sewing needle with yarn. Starting at the bottom and working from right to left, place the needle under the loop of the first stitch on both pieces and draw the yarn through. Move up one stitch and repeat this process going from left to right. Continue to zigzag loosely from edge to edge. Pull the yarn tight every inch (2.5 cm) or so, allowing the edges to join together. A woven seam gives a flatter finish than a backstitch seam and works better when sewing together baby garments and fine work.

Edge finishes

Edge finishes can be worked directly into the crochet fabric. Single crochet edging is used mainly for finishing necklines and borders on garments and it can be worked in a contrasting color of yarn. Crab stitch edging is more hard-wearing due to the small knots of yarn made along the row. It can be worked directly into the edge of a piece of crochet fabric, as shown, or several rows of single crochet can be worked first to act as a foundation. Picot edgings offer a more decorative finish.

Single crochet edging

Single crochet is a useful and flexible edge finish. Working from right to left, make a row of ordinary single crochet stitches (see page 21) into the edge of the crochet fabric, spacing the stitches evenly along the edge.

Crab stitch edging

Also known as reverse double crochet, this stitch makes a strong, fairly rigid edging with an attractive texture. Unlike most other crochet techniques, this stitch is worked from left to right along the row.

1 Keeping the yarn to the left, insert the hook from front to back into the next stitch and wrap the yarn over the hook.

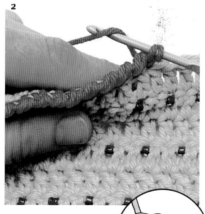

2 Draw the loop through the stitch from back to front so that there are now two loops on the hook. Finish by wrapping the yarn over the hook again, then draw the yarn through both loops to complete the stitch.

Picot edging

This stitch makes a delicate edge with tiny protruding loops of yarn. Work a foundation row of single crochet and then turn the work.

1 Work three chain stitches, then work a slip stitch into the third chain from the hook. This makes one picot.

2 Skip the next stitch, then work a slip stitch into the following stitch. Repeat from the beginning of step 1 and continue doing so all along the edge.

Wearable Accessories

Project 1: Beaded ruffle scarf

This gloriously tactile spiral scarf is very easy to crochet and looks fabulous. It's a great way to practise your increasing technique. It is crocheted in two different weights, the lambswool-and-kid-mohair aran-weight yarn is edged with a lightweight cobweb kid-mohair-and-silk yarn with glass beads along the outer edge.

before you start

MATERIALS
Yarn A: 3 x 50 g (1.75 oz) balls aran-weight lambswool-and-kid-mohair blend (approximately 153 yds/140 m per ball) in red
Yarn B: 1 x 25 g (0.8 oz) ball laceweight 2-ply kid-mohair-and-silk blend (approximately 230 yds/210 m per ball) in deep red
Approximately 110 multicolored large glass beads

HOOK SIZE
U.S. J-10 (6.0 mm)

GAUGE/TENSION
Not applicable for this project.

FINISHED SIZE
Approximately 74 in. (190 cm) long and 4.5 in. (11 cm) wide.

ABBREVIATIONS
beg—beginning
bsc—beaded single crochet
ch—chain
rnd—round
sc—single crochet
sp—space
ss—slip stitch
st(s)—stitch(es)
tr—treble
yo—yarn over

SCARF PATTERN
Using yarn A, ch 161.

Rnd 1: Sc into second ch from the hook and into each ch, working 2 sc into last ch st. Working in remaining loops of beginning chain already worked, sc into each ch across, working 2 sc into the last ch st. Join with sl st to first sc of rnd.
Rnd 2: Ch 3, work 2 tr into every sc. Join with sl st into top of beg ch 3.

Rnd 3: Ch 3, work 3 tr into each of the next 320 sts (first half of round). Finish off yarn A. Do not turn. Thread beads onto yarn B. Join yarn B with a slip stitch to base of last tr worked. Working in the remaining sts of rnd 2, bsc into next tr, *sc in next 2 sts, bsc in next st, repeat from * across, ending with sl st to base of beginning tr of rnd.

Break off yarn and weave in ends.

Project 2: Lace-effect shawl

Wrap yourself up in this luxurious, elegant shawl. Each square is worked separately using combinations of a DK tweed wool in a soft green and a variety of tonal shades in a 2-ply kid-mohair-and-silk blend. This creates a wonderful color change throughout. The squares are simply crocheted together with the cobweb 2-ply and beads placed throughout.

before you start

MATERIALS

Yarn A: 5 skeins DK-weight merino wool, alpaca, viscose mix (approximately 192 yds/175 m per 50g (1.75 oz) ball) in olive green
Yarn B: 1 skein worsted-weight kid-mohair-and-silk blend (approximately 230 yds/210 m per 50 g (1.75 oz) ball) in pale blue
Yarn C: 1 skein worsted-weight kid-mohair-and-silk blend (approximately 230 yds/210 m per 50 g (1.75 oz) ball) in green
Yarn D: 1 skein worsted-weight kid-mohair-and-silk blend (approximately 230 yds/210 m per 50 g (1.75 oz) ball) in black
500 silver-lined, clear glass beads

HOOK SIZE

U.S. G-6 (4.0 mm)

GAUGE/TENSION

4 in. (10 cm) per motif

FINISHED SIZE

48 in. (122 cm) by 16 in. (40 cm)

ABBREVIATIONS

beg—beginning
bsc—beaded single crochet
ch—chain
dc—double crochet
lp—loop
sl st—slip stitch
sc—single crochet
sp—space
ws—wrong side

MOTIF

Make 24 motifs with yarns A and B held together, 12 motifs with yarns A and C held together, and 12 motifs with yarns A and D held together.
Ch 6, join to form a ring.

Rnd 1: Ch 6 (counts as dc plus 3 ch), *3 dc into ring, ch 1, rep from * twice more, 2 dc into ring, join with sl st into third ch of beg ch 6.

Rnd 2: Sl st into next ch sp, ch 6, 3 dc into same sp, *ch 1, (3 dc, ch 3, 3 dc) into next ch sp, rep from * twice more, 2 dc into next ch sp, join with sl st into third ch of beg ch 6.

Rnd 3: Sl st into next ch sp, ch 6, 3 dc into same sp, *ch 1, 3 dc into next sp, ch 1, (3 dc, ch 3, 3 dc into corner sp, rep from * twice more, ch 1, 3 dc into next sp, ch 1, 2 dc into next space, join with sl st into third ch of beg ch 6.
Fasten off.

JOINING

Thread beads onto yarn B. Join motifs according to the diagram below.

Hold motifs with ws together and yarn B motif facing you. Join yarn A with sl st in upper right corner lp of yarn B motif. Bsc in same lp, ch 1. Bsc in corresponding corner lp of yarn C motif behind. *Ch 1, bsc in next ch lp of yarn B motif, ch 1, bsc in next ch lp of yarn C motif. Rep from * until upper left corner of yarn C motif has been worked. Fasten off.

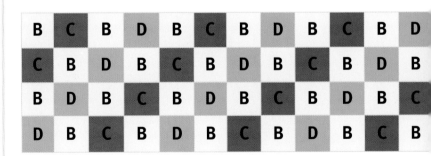

New skills/Joining squares together

When you have lots of squares to join, it is best to work in sections. Join individual squares to make strips, and then join these strips together. Zig-zag from one square to the next using a mixture of chains and beaded single crochet techniques.

1 Thread all beads onto yarn in sequence. Hold squares with right sides outside. Join yarn at top upper right hand corner of front square and work 1 sc.

2 Work 1 bsc into same place as sc, work 1 ch, then 1 bsc into top corner of square that is held to the back. Work 1 ch.

3 Work 1 bsc into first sp from corner of front square, 1 ch, 1 bsc into top of center double of back square. Rep steps 1 and 2, moving along 1 st/sp each time.

Project 3: Wrist warmers

These wrist warmers are a pretty yet practical piece, a fun and funky way to add your own touch to an outfit. Worked mainly in a kid-mohair-and-silk 2-ply yarn, they are soft, light, and cozy. Try making them in vibrant contrasting colors. They are perfect for wearing with a jacket and jumper, keeping you warm, but letting you wriggle your fingers, while the beaded trim adds that finishing touch.

before you start

MATERIALS
Yarn A: laceweight kid-mohair-and-silk blend (approximately 109 yds/100 m per 0.8 oz/25 g) in green
Yarn B: 1 x 50 g (1.75 oz) ball sport-weight cotton (approximately 123 yds/113 m per ball) in teal
Approximately 200 small black beads

HOOK SIZE
U.S. E-4 (3.5 mm)

GAUGE/TENSION
5 groups of crossed dc to 4 in. (10 cm)

FINISHED SIZE
8 in. (20 cm) diameter, 5 in. (12.5 cm) long

ABBREVIATIONS
bsc—beaded single crochet
ch—chain
dc—double crochet
rnd—round
rs—right side
sc—single crochet
sk—skip
ws—wrong side

MITTEN
Make 2.

Row 1: Using yarn A, ch 44. Dc in third ch from hook. *Sk one ch, dc in next 3 ch, work dc in skipped ch to surround last 3 dc worked. Repeat from * across. Dc in last ch, turn (42 sts including turning ch).
Rows 2–7: Ch 2 (counts as first dc), *skip next dc, dc in next 3 sts, work dc in skipped st to surround last 3 dc worked. Repeat from * across. Dc in last dc, turn. Break off yarn and sew in ends. Sew side seam, leaving a 1.25-in. (3-cm) opening for thumb.

EDGING
Rnd 1 (ws): Using yarn B and with wrong side of work facing, join with sl st in last row of mitten, at seam. Ch 1, bsc in each st around. Join with sl st to first bsc of rnd.
Rnd 2 (rs): Ch 1, sc in each st around. Join with sl st to first sc.
Rnd 3: Ch 1, bsc in each st around.

Finish off.

Project 4: Pashmina

This beautifully cozy, sumptuous pashmina is made with a comforting combination of a DK tweed yarn in a soft gray and a variety of tonal shades in a 2-ply kid-mohair-and-silk blend. The beads are placed throughout the stripe pattern to add an extra-special touch. It's a perfect accompaniment to any outfit—winter or summer!

STRIPE PATTERN

Using yarn A, ch 52.

Row 1: Dc into fourth ch from the hook, and into each of the next 2 ch. Work sdc as follows: yo, insert hook into last unworked st before the 3 dc group just made, yo, draw up a loop surrounding these sts so as not to crush the 3 dc group, [yo, draw through 2 loops] twice (sdc completed). *Skip 1 ch, dc in each of the next 3 ch, sdc, repeat from * 11 more times, ending with dc in the last st. Break off yarn A and begin with yarn B.

Row 2: Ch 2, turn. Dc into second dc of row, dc in each of the next 2 sts, bsdc as follows: yo, bring bead up to hook, insert hook into last unworked st before the 3 dc group just made, yo, draw up a loop surrounding the 3 dc group as before, [yo, draw through 2 loops] twice (bsdc completed). *Skip 1 dc from the previous row, dc in each of the next 3 sts, bsdc, repeat from * 11 more times, ending with dc in the last st.

Row 3: As row 2. Break off yarn and begin with yarn A.

Row 4: Ch 2, turn. Dc into each of the next 3 sts, sdc * skip 1 st from the row below, dc in each of the next 3 sts, bsdc, repeat from * 11 times, ending with dc in the last st. Break off yarn A and change to yarn C.

Rows 5–6: Work as rows 2–3.

Row 7: As row 4, changing to yarn B at end of row.

Rows 8–21: Repeat rows 2–7 twice more, then repeat rows 2–3 once.

before you start

MATERIALS

Yarn A: 3 x 50 g (1.75 oz) balls of aran-weight lambswool-and-kid-mohair blend (approximately 97 yds/89 m per ball) in gray

Yarn B: 1 x 25 g (0.8 oz) ball of laceweight 2-ply kid-mohair-and-silk blend (approximately 237 yds/217 m per ball) in rose

Yarn C: 1 x 25 g (0.8 oz) ball of laceweight 2-ply kid-mohair-and-silk blend (approximately 237 yds/217 m per ball) in blue

Approximately 340 purple glass beads

HOOK SIZE

U.S. J-10 (6.0 mm) hook

GAUGE/TENSION

13 stitches and 4 rows to 4 in. (10 cm) over border stripe pattern

13 stitches and 5.5 rows to 4 in. (10 cm) over solid pattern

FINISHED SIZE

12.5 in. (32 cm) wide by 51.5 in. (131 cm) long

ABBREVIATIONS

bsdc—beaded spike double crochet

ch—chain

dc—double crochet

sdc—spike double crochet

st(s)—stitches

yo—yarn over

PREPARATION

Thread 192 beads onto yarn B and 144 beads onto yarn C

SOLID FABRIC PATTERN

Rows 22–53: Continuing with yarn A, ch 2, turn. Dc into each of the next 3 sts, sdc * skip 1 st from the row below, dc in each of the next 3 sts, bsdc, repeat from * 11 times, ending with dc in the last st.

STRIPE PATTERN

Rows 54–74: Break off yarn A and change to yarn B. Repeat rows 2–7 three more times, then rows 2–4 once, ending by finishing off stripe border pattern: yarn A (without joining a new color).

FINISHING

Draw all beads through to the right side of wrap. Weave in all loose ends, and block to finished size.

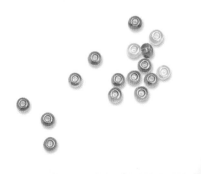

Project 5: Beaded string bag

This design is a real blast from the past. The DK cotton and chunky woode beads give a boho retro feel. The textural wooden beads stand out from the matt DK cotton, the open mesh netting crochet stitch adds to the look. The simple drawstring loop handle can be easily extended so you can strap the bag across the body and go; perfect for fun at the beach or taking your shopping back from the store.

before you start

MATERIALS

2 x 50 g (1.75 oz) balls (approximately 97 yds/89 m per ball) DK-weight cotton in turquoise
Beads: 127 pink 6-mm wooden beads
127 purple 8-mm wooden beads
127 natural 10-mm wooden beads

HOOK SIZE

U.S. G-6 (4.5 mm) hook

GAUGE/TENSION

With chain loops fully stretched to form points, first round should measure approximately 3 in. (7.5 cm) diameter

FINISHED SIZE

Laid flat, not including handles, bag measures 14 in. (35.5 cm) wide by 16 in. (40.5 cm) high

ABBREVIATIONS

bsc—beaded single crochet
ch—chain
dc—double crochet
hk—hook
lp(s)—loop(s)
rnd—round
sc—single crochet
sl st—slip stitch

BAG PATTERN

Thread beads onto yarn in repeating sequence pink, purple, then natural. Approx 276 will complete the first ball of yarn.
Ch 8, join to farthest ch from hk with sl st to form a ring.

Rnd 1: Ch 1, work 1 sc into ring, *ch 9, sc 1 into ring, rep from * 20 more times. Sl st into first sc. (21 lps)
Rnd 2: Sl st into first 4 ch of ch-9 lp, ch 1, *bsc into lp as follows: bring bead up to

hook and work sc as normal (bsc completed), rep from * 20 more times, sl st into first sc to close round.
Rnds 3–19: Rep rnd 2 another 17 times. (Hint: the bag can be lengthened by adding reps of the final round, but remember that more beads would be needed.)

HANDLE

Ch 7.
Row 1: Dc into the third ch from hk and into each ch to end.

Row 2: Ch 2, dc into each st across.
Rows 3–80: Rep row 2.

FINISHING

Weave in all loose ends.
Thread strap in and out of ch lps of the last round of the bag.
Making sure that the strap is not twisted, sew the ends of the strap together.

New skills/placing beads in sequence

When more than one color or type of bead is being used in a project, you have to remember to thread them on in sequence. Most patterns will give you this information, but remember that the first bead on will be the last bead worked.

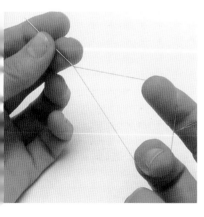

1 Thread sewing needle with sewing cotton thread and tie ends in a knot to form a loop.

2 Place beads in small tubs and lay out in front in sequence as indicated in pattern.

3 Place yarn being used through sewing cotton loop and begin threading on beads in sequence.

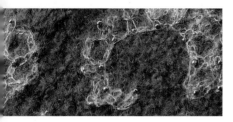

Project 6: Shoulder bag

This bag is very structured—the main body of the bag and handle are heavily felted to add a utility feel, and the shaping of the strap and the color changes all add to the effect. The crotcheted motifs, worked in a soft 2-ply kid-mohair-and-silk, soften the look, and the beads add depth. The motifs may look complicated, but they are a simple twist on the picot mesh stitch.

BAG PANEL

Make 2.

Using yarn A and larger hook, ch 30.

Row 1: Dc in third ch from hook and in each ch across. Ch 2, turn.

Rows 2–8: Dc into each st across. Ch2, turn.

Row 9: Dc into each st across. Change to yarn B. Ch 2, turn.

Row 10: Dc into each st across. Change to yarn A. Ch 2, turn.

Row 11: Repeat row 2.

Row 12: Repeat row 9.

Rows 13–14: Repeat row 2.

Row 15: Dc into each st across. Finish off and sew in yarn ends.

Make a second bag panel identical to the first.

With wrong sides facing, sew panels together along one side seam.

HANDLE

Open out newly joined seam.

With right sides facing, join yarn A with a sl st at top edge, 9 sts before the side seam.

Row 1: Ch 2, dc in each of the next 18 sts. Change to yarn B, ch 2, turn.

Row 2: Work dc decrease as follows: yo, insert hook into next st, yo and draw up a loop, yo and draw through 2 loops, (2 loops still on hook), yo, insert hook into next stitch, yo and draw up a loop, yo, draw through 2 loops, yo, and draw through remaining 3 loops. Dc decrease made. Dc in each of the next 14 sts, work dc decrease. Ch 2, turn.

Row 3: Dc decrease, dc in the next 12 sts, dc decrease. Change to yarn A, ch 2, turn.

---

before you start

MATERIALS

Yarn A: 2 x 100 g (3.5 oz) balls bulky weight yarn in feltable 100% wool (not superwash) approximately 87.5 yds/80 m per ball) in smoky gray

Yarn B: 1 x 100 g (3.5 oz) ball bulky weight yarn in feltable 100% wool (not superwash) approximately 87.5 yds/80 m per ball) in black

Yarn C: 1 x 25 g (0.8 oz) ball kid-mohair-and-silk blend laceweight yarn (approximately 230 yds/210 m per ball) in lilac

Approximately 150 glass beads

HOOK SIZES

U.S. M/N-13 (9.0 mm) and U.S. E-4 (3.5 mm)

GAUGE/TENSION

Not critical since project is felted, but not tighter than 8 sts per 4 in. (10 cm)

FINISHED SIZE AFTER FELTING

Body of bag measures 12.5 in. (32 cm) by 9.5 in. (24 cm) Total length including handle measures 23 in. (58.5 cm)

ABBREVIATIONS

bch—beaded chain

bp—beaded picot

ch—chain

dc—double crochet

sc—single crochet

sl st—slip stitch

st(s)—stitch(es)

yo—yarn over

Row 4: Dc decrease, dc in the next 10 sts, dc decrease. Change to yarn B, ch 2, turn.

Row 5: Dc decrease, dc in the next 9 sts, dc decrease. Ch 2, turn.

Rows 6–8: Dc in each st across. Ch 2, turn.

Row 9: Dc decrease, dc in the next 7 sts, dc decrease. Ch 2, turn.

Rows 10–25: Dc in each st across. Ch 2, turn.

Row 26: Work 2 dc into the first st, dc each of the next 7 sts, 2 dc into last st. Ch 2, turn.

Row 27: Work 2 dc into the first st, dc each of the next 9 sts, 2 dc into the last st. Finish off and sew in ends.

ASSEMBLY

Turn bag with right sides together and sew remaining side seam.

Stitch end of handle into place.

FELTING INSTRUCTIONS

Place bag in washing machine along with an old pair of blue jeans or other sturdy fabric. Avoid towels as these can leave fibers on your bag. Wash in warm water (detergent optional), agitating until bag shrinks to finished size. Note that this may take more than one wash cycle. Once bag is felted to finished size, lay flat to dry.

Shoulder bag motifs

MOTIF 1

Make 2.

Thread 6 beads onto yarn.

Using yarn C and smaller hook, ch 20.

Row 1: Sc into eighth ch from hook, make beaded picot (bp) as follows: ch 1, bch, ch, sl st into base of sc just made. Beaded picot made. *Ch 5, skip 3 ch, bp, repeat from * 2 more times. Turn to work next row into foundation chain.

Row 2: *Ch 5, sc into ch 3 space, bp, repeat from * once more.

Fasten off.

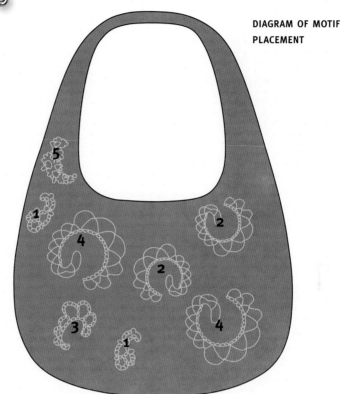

DIAGRAM OF MOTIF PLACEMENT

MOTIF 2

Make 2.

Thread 26 beads onto yarn.

Using yarn C and smaller hook bch, (ch 3, bc) 9 times, ch 4.

Row 1: Sc into eighth ch from hook, bp, (ch 7, skip 3 ch, sc, bp) 5 times, (ch 5, skip 3 ch, sc, bp) 3 times. Turn.

Row 2: (Ch 5, sc into ch space, bp) 5 times. Turn.

Row 3: (Ch 5, sc into ch space, bpc) twice.

Fasten off.

MOTIF 3

Make 1.

Thread 14 beads onto yarn.

Using yarn C and smaller hook, bch, (ch 3, bc) 6 times, ch 4.

Row 1: Sc into eighth ch from hook, bp, ch 5, skip 3 ch, sc, bp, ch 7, skip 3 ch, sc, bp, ch 9, skip 3 ch, sc, bp, ch 7, skip 3 ch, sc, bp, ch 5, skip 3 ch, sc, bp, ch 3, skip 3 ch, sc, bp.

Fasten off.

MOTIF 4

Make 2.

Thread 27 beads onto yarn.

Using yarn C and smaller hook bch, (ch 3, bc) 9 times, ch 4.

Row 1: Sc into eighth ch from hook, (ch 5, sc, bp, skip 3 ch) 5 times, (ch 7, sc, bp, skip 3 ch) 3 times, (ch 5, sc, bp, skip 3 ch) twice. Turn.

Row 2: (Ch 5, sc into next ch space, bp) 3 times, (ch 7, sc into next ch space, bp) 3 times.

Fasten off.

MOTIF 5

Make 1.

Thread 7 beads onto yarn.

Using yarn C and smaller hook ch 24.

Row 1: Sc into eighth ch from hook, bp, (ch 5, sc, bp, skip 3 ch) twice, ch 7, sc, bp, skip 3 ch, ch 7, sc, bp. Turn.

Row 2: (Ch 7, sc into next ch space, bp) twice, ch 5, sc into ch space, bp.

Fasten off.

Project 7: Evening bag

This little bag is perfect for a night out on the town. The dark chocolate background sparkles with bright beads in a modern color combination. Made out of two rectangles with a large slash for a handle, the all-over beaded fabric adds weight and body to the medium-weight cotton bag. It is a great project to do if you've just mastered the basics.

before you start

MATERIALS

2 x 50 g (1.75 oz) balls sport-weight cotton (approx 123 yds/ 113 m per ball) in brown
240 dark turquoise glass beads
280 green glass beads
220 silvery green glass beads

HOOK SIZE

U.S. E-4 (3.5 mm) hook

GAUGE/TENSION

19 stiches and 24 rows over 4 in. (10 cm) in single crochet.

FINISHED SIZE

7.5 in. (19 cm) wide by 7.75 in. (20 cm) high

ABBREVIATIONS

bsc—beaded single crochet
ch—chain
sc—single crochet
sl st—slip stitch
st(s)—stitch(es)

FRONT PANEL

Thread beads onto yarn in sequence, repeating (40 green, 40 dark turquoise, 40 silvery green) 5 times, then 40 green, 40 dark turquoise, 40 green, and 20 silvery green.
Ch 36.

Row 1 (right side): Sc into second ch from hook and in each ch to end (35 sts). Ch 1, turn.
Row 2: Bsc into each st across. Ch 1, turn.
Row 3: Sc into each st across. Ch 1, turn.
Rows 4–33: Repeat rows 2 and 3 to form beaded stripe pattern.
Row 34: Repeat row 2.

Make slash handle

Row 35: Sc into each of the first 10 bsc, Ch 15, skip 15 bsc of the previous row, sc into each of the last 10 sts of row. Ch 1, turn.
Row 36: Bsc into each of the first 10 sc of the previous row, bsc into each of the 15 ch sts, bsc into each of the last 10 sc. Ch 1, turn.
Row 37: Sc into each st across. Ch 1, turn.
Row 38: Bsc in each st across.
Rows 39–42: Repeat rows 37 and 38 twice.
Row 43: Repeat row 37.

Fasten off.

BACK PANEL

Ch 36.

Row 1 (right side): Sc into second ch from the hook and in each ch to end (35 sts). Ch 1, turn.
Rows 2–34: Sc into each st across.

Make slash handle

Row 35: Sc into each of the first sc, ch 15, skip 15 sc of the previous row, sc into each of the last 10 sts of row. Ch 1, turn.
Row 36: Sc into each of the first 10 sc of the previous row, sc into each of the 15 ch, sc into each of the last 10 sc. Ch 1, turn.
Rows 37–42: Sc into each st across. Ch 1, turn.
Row 43: Sc into each st across. Finish off.

FINISHING

Weave all loose ends into fabric.
Block panels to finished size.
With wrong sides together, sew along side and bottom edges.

Project 8 : Flower pin corsage

This pretty piece can be pinned onto anything; use it to jazz up a hat, jacket, or bag. Delightfully feminine, the frilly kid-mohair-and-silk beaded petals almost froth and shimmer. Have fun creating your own color combinations.

before you start

MATERIALS

Yarn A: 25 g (0.8 oz) ball sock-weight 100% wool (approximately 120 yds/110 m per ball) in green
Yarn B: 25 g (0.8 oz) ball sock-weight 100% wool (approximately 120 yds/110 m per ball) in purple
Yarn C: 25 g (0.8 oz) ball laceweight kid-mohair-and-silk blend (approximately 230 yds/ 210 m per ball) in gray
120 black glass beads.
One pin backing

HOOK SIZE

U.S. E-4 (3.5 mm)

GAUGE/TENSION

Round 1 laid flat measures 0.5 in. (1.3 cm) across.

FINISHED SIZE

5 in. (13 cm), by 3.5 in. (9 cm)

ABBREVIATIONS

bch—beaded chain
ch—chain
dc—double crochet
dtr—double treble crochet
lkdtr—linked double treble crochet
rnd—round
sc—single crochet
sl st—slip stitch
tr—treble crochet
yo—yarn over

FLOWER PATTERN

Rnd 1: With yarn A, ch 3. Insert hook through second ch from hook, yo, draw up lp, insert hook in ring, yo and draw up a lp, complete dc as normal. *Insert hook down through horizontal lp around post of last dc made, yo, draw up lp, insert hook in ring, yo, draw up a lp and complete dc as normal. Rep from * a total of 5 times. Sl st to top of beginning ch 3 (6 sts).

Rnd 2: Ch 5. Insert hook through second ch from hook, yo, draw up lp, [insert hook in next ch, yo, draw up lp] twice (4 lps on hook). Insert hook in next st, yo, draw up lp. Complete dtr as normal. *Work lkdtr: insert hook down through uppermost of 3 horizontal lps around the post of last st made, yo, draw up lp. [Insert hook down through next horizontal lp, yo, and draw up lp] twice, insert hook in same st as before, yo, and draw up lp. Complete dtr as normal. Lkdtr made. Work 2 lkdtr in each st 5 times, join with sl st to top of ch 5 (12 sts).

Change to yarn B.

Rnd 3: Ch 1, Sc into each st around, join with sl st to first sc.
Rnd 4: Rep rnd 3.

Rnd 5: Ch 1, 2 sc into first st, 3 sc into each st around, ending sc into same st as first 2 sc of round, join with sl st to first sc of round (36 sts).
Rnd 6: Ch 3, (counts as first dc), 2 dc into first st, 3 dc into each st around, sl st into top of ch 3 (108 sts).

Fasten off yarn B.

Thread beads onto yarn C. With ws facing, join yarn C with sl st in any st of last round.
Rnd 7: Ch 1, sc into same st, * ch 2, bch, ch 2, sc into next st, rep from * around ending sl st into first sc of round (108 bch lps).

Fasten off yarn C.

STEM

Rejoin yarn A in ch base of first round of stem. Ch 20, sc into second ch from hook and into each ch across. Sl st into base of rnd 1 on opposite side of round.

Fasten off

Fold stem double and stitch sides together Sew on pin backing.

New skills/working a linked double treble

The linked double treble stitch technique used in this project is essentially the same as a normal double treble but is worked by going into the stem of previous stitch or turning chain. In doing this we form a solid fabric but can still have the depth of the longer stitches. When working first linked double treble, work into the turning chain.

 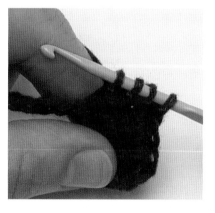 

1 Insert hook into uppermost of 3 horizontal lps around the stem of the last st made, yo and draw through.

2 Insert hook into the next horizontal loops around the stem of the last st made, yo and draw through, rep once more (4 lps on hook).

3 Insert hook into next st, yo and draw through. Yo and draw through first 2 lps, rep yo and drawing through 2 lps until 1 lp left on hook.

Project 9: Beaded beanie

This is a great project to practise your increasing techniques in the round. The rounded yarn adds something special to simple textures such as double crochet. The beaded edge of the beanie is simple and effective; try threading on lots of differently colored beads and see how the colors emerge.

before you start

MATERIALS

2 x 50 g (1.75 oz) balls 50% cotton, 50% wool, DK-weight yarn (approximately 123 yds/113 m per ball) in ecru
Approximately 300 matt green beads

HOOK SIZE

U.S. E-4 (3.5 mm)

GAUGE/TENSION

17 sts and 14 rows to 4 in. (10 cm)

ABBREVIATIONS

bhdc—beaded half double crochet
ch—chain
hdc—half double crochet
rnd—round
sl st—slip stitch
st(s)—stitch(es)
ws—wrong side

PATTERN

Ch 4, sl st in farthest ch from hook to form a ring.

Rnd 1: Ch 2, make 8 hdc into ring, sl st into first hdc of rnd (8 sts).
Rnd 2: Ch 2, work 2 hdc into each st around, ending with sl st into first hdc (16 sts).
Rnd 3: Ch 2, *2 hdc into next st, 1 hdc into next st, repeat from * around, ending with sl st into first hdc (24 sts).
Rnd 4: Ch 2, *2 hdc into next st, hdc into each of the next 2 sts, repeat from *, ending with sl st into first hdc (32 sts).
Rnd 5: Ch 2, *2 hdc into next st, hdc into each of the next 3 sts, repeat from *, ending with sl st into first hdc (40 sts).
Rnd 6: Ch 2, *2 hdc into next st, hdc into each of the next 4 sts, repeat from *, ending with sl st into first hdc (48 sts).
Rnd 7: Ch 2, *2 hdc into next st, hdc into each of the next 5 sts, repeat from *, ending with sl st into first hdc (56 sts).
Rnd 8: Ch 2, *2 hdc into next st, hdc into each of the next 6 sts, repeat from *, ending with sl st into first hdc (64 sts).
Rnd 9: Ch 2, *2 hdc into next st, hdc into each of the next 7 sts, repeat from *, ending with sl st into first hdc (72 sts).

Rnd 10: Ch 2, *2 hdc into next st, hdc into each of the next 8 sts, repeat from *, ending with sl st into first hdc (80 sts).
Rnd 11: Ch 2, *2 hdc into next st, hdc into each of the next 9 sts, repeat from *, ending with sl st into first hdc (88 sts).
Rnds 12–22: Ch 2, hdc into each st around, ending with sl st into first hdc.
At end of rnd 22, break off yarn.
Thread beads onto yarn. Turn work so ws is facing. Join with sl st in any st of rnd 22.
Rnd 23: Ch 2, bhdc into each st around, sl st into first st of rnd.
Rnd 24: Ch 2, hdc into each st around, sl st into first st of rnd.
Rnds 25–28: Repeat rows 23 and 24 twice more. At end of rnd 28, break off yarn.

With rs of work facing, join with sl st into beginning ring of rnd 1 (at top of beanie).
Rnd 29: Ch 2, work 5 hdc evenly around ring in spaces between sts of rnd 1, sl st to first hdc of this rnd.
Rnd 30: Ch 2, work one bhdc into each st of previous rnd, pulling beads to front of work. Sl st into first bhdc to join.

Project 10: Twenties-inspired scarf

The beaded crochet loop trim on this scarf gives it a real 1920s-flapper feel. Crocheted and beaded in soft appealing greens, the lightweight kid-mohair-and-silk yarn used is soft and light to the touch and the beaded ends add a great swing!

before you start

MATERIALS
2 x 25 g (0.8 oz) balls kid-mohair-and-silk blend laceweight 2-ply yarn (approximately 237 yds/217 m per ball) in soft green
Approximately 940 green glass beads

HOOK SIZE
U.S. G-6 (4.5 mm)

GAUGE/TENSION
Approximately 9 beaded loops per 4 in. (10 cm) width
21 stitches and 8 rows to 4 in. (10 cm)

FINISHED SIZE
4.25 in. (11 cm) wide by 52 in. (132 cm) long
Note that the weight of beaded fringe may cause scarf to stretch longer and narrower.

ABBREVIATIONS
bdc—beaded double crochet
ch—chain
dc—double crochet
hdc—half double crochet
lp—loop
lphdc—loop half double crochet
rep—rep
sl st—slip stitch
st(s)—stitch(es)
ws—wrong side
yo—yarn over

SCARF PANEL
Make two panels.
Thread 470 beads onto yarn.
Ch 23.
Loop fringe.

Row 1: Hdc into third ch from hook and in each ch to end (21 sts).
Row 2: Ch 2, turn. Hdc into first hdc. *Make lphdc as follows—bring 10 beads up to the hook, yo, insert hook into into next st and pull up a lp, yo and draw through all 3 lps on hook (lphdc completed). Hdc in the next st. Rep from * 8 more times.
Row 3: Ch 2, turn. Hdc into each hdc across.
Row 4: Ch 2, turn. Hdc into first hdc, *hdc into next st, lphdc, rep from * 8 more times. Hdc in each of the last 2 sts.
Row 5–7: Rep rows 2–4.

MAIN SCARF FABRIC
Row 8: Ch 2, turn. Dc in each st across.
Row 9: Ch 2, turn. Dc in each of the next 2 sts. *Work bdc as follows—slide bead up to crochet hook and work dc as normal (bdc completed). Dc in each of the next 4 sts, bdc in the next st, rep from * 3 more times, ending row with bdc, 2 dc.

Thread beads onto yarn C. With ws facing join yarn C with sl st in any st of last round.
Rnd 11: Ch 2, dc in each of the next 5 sts, *bdc in the next st, dc in each of the next 4 sts, rep from * once more, bdc in next st, dc in each of the last 4 sts.
Rnd 12: As row 8.
Rnd 13–60: Rep rows 9–12 another 12 times.

Next row: Hdc in each st across.
For panel 1 only
Break off yarn at this point.
For panel 2 only
Row 61 (panel 2 only): Rep row 8
Row 62 (panel 2 only): Rep row 9.
Fasten off.

FINISHING
Sew all loose ends into fabric. Block to desired measurements.
Sew center seam of scarf with a flat stitch.

New skills/working a beaded crochet loop

This loop edge looks much more complicated than it actually is—whether you are placing 5 or 10 beads the same technique is used. The more beads you have the longer the loop will be.

1 Work in pattern to required position. Bring the required amount of beads up to the crochet hook.

2 Insert hook into next stitch and complete as normal.

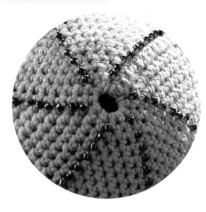

Project 11: Beaded beret

Crocheted in a woollen 4-ply rounded yarn, the increasing and decreasing techniques used to create the beret are used to place the beads throughout. The beads highlight the pattern—and watching the beaded spiral pattern emerge as you crochet is very satisfying!

PATTERN

Ch 6, sl st in farthest ch from hook to form a ring.

Rnd 1: Ch 1, work 12 sc into ring, join with sl st into first sc (12 sts).

Rnd 2: Ch 1, bsc into the same st, *sc in the next st, (sc, bsc) into the next st, rep from * around, join with sl st into first st of rnd (18 sts and 6 beads).

Rnd 3: Ch 1, bsc into same st, *sc into each of the next 2 sts, (sc, bsc) into the next st, rep from * around, ending with sc in same st as beginning of rnd and sl st into first bsc (24 sts).

Rnd 4: Ch 1, bsc into same st, *sc into each of the next 3 sts, (sc, bsc) into the next st, rep from * around, ending with sc in same st as beginning of rnd and sl st into first bsc (30 sts).

Rnd 5: Ch 1, bsc into same st, *sc into each of the next 4 sts, (sc, bsc) into the next st, rep from * around, ending with sc in same st as beginning of rnd and sl st into first bsc (36 sts).

Rnd 6: Ch 1, bsc into same st, *sc into each of the next 5 sts, (sc, bsc) into the next st, rep from * around, ending with sc in same st as beginning of rnd and sl st into first bsc (42 sts).

Rnd 7: Ch 1, bsc into same st, *sc into each of the next 6 sts, (sc, bsc) into the next st, rep from * around, ending with sc in same st as beginning of rnd and sl st into first bsc (48 sts).

Rnd 8: Ch 1, bsc into same st, *sc into each of the next 7 sts, (sc, bsc) into the

before you start

MATERIALS

2 x 50 g (1.75 oz) balls sport-weight 100% wool (approximately 191 yds/175 m per ball) in pale blue Approximately 250 glass beads in pewter

HOOK SIZE

U.S. E-4 (3.5 mm)

GAUGE/TENSION

24 stitches and 27 rows to 4 in. (10 cm)

FINISHED SIZE

Approximately 9.5 in. (24 cm) diameter

ABBREVIATIONS

bsc—beaded single crochet
bsc dec—beaded single crochet decrease
ch—chain
lp(s)—loop(s)
rep—repeat
sc—single crochet
sl st—slip stitch
st(s)—stitch(es)
yo—yarn over

next st, rep from * around, ending with sc in same st as beginning of rnd and sl st into first bsc (54 sts).

Rnd 9: Ch 1, bsc into same st, *sc into each of the next 8 sts, (sc, bsc) into the next st, rep from * around, ending with sc in same st as beginning of rnd and sl st into first bsc (60 sts).

Rnd 10: Ch 1, bsc into same st, *sc into each of the next 9 sts, (sc, bsc) into the next st, rep from * around, ending with sc in same st as beginning of rnd and sl st into first bsc (66 sts).

Rnd 11: Ch 1, bsc into same st, *sc into each of the next 10 sts, (sc, bsc) into the next st, rep from * around, ending with sc in same st as beginning of rnd and sl st into first bsc (72 sts).

Rnd 12: Ch 1, bsc into same st, *sc into

each of the next 11 sts, (sc, bsc) into the next st, rep from * around, ending with sc in same st as beginning of rnd and sl st into first bsc (78 sts).

Rnd 13: Ch 1, bsc into same st, *sc into each of the next 12 sts, (sc, bsc) into the next st, rep from * around, ending with sc in same st as beginning of rnd and sl st into first bsc (84 sts).

Rnd 14: Ch 1, bsc into same st, *sc into each of the next 13 sts, (sc, bsc) into the next st, rep from * around, ending with sc in same st as beginning of rnd and sl st into first bsc (90 sts).

Rnd 15: Ch 1, bsc into same st, *sc into each of the next 14 sts, (sc, bsc) into the next st, rep from * around, ending with sc in same st as beginning of rnd and sl st into first bsc (96 sts).

Rnd 16: Ch 1, bsc into same st, *sc into each of the next 15 sts, (sc, bsc) into the next st, rep from * around, ending with sc in same st as beginning of rnd and sl st into first bsc (102 sts).

Rnd 17: Ch 1, bsc into same st, *sc into each of the next 16 sts, (sc, bsc) into the next st, rep from * around, ending with sc in same st as beginning of rnd and sl st into first bsc (108 sts).

Rnd 18: Ch 1, bsc into same st, *sc into each of the next 17 sts, (sc, bsc) into the next st, rep from * around, ending with sc in same st as beginning of rnd and sl st into first bsc (114 sts).

Rnd 19: Ch 1, bsc into same st, *sc into each of the next 18 sts, (sc, bsc) into the next st, rep from * around, ending with sc in same st as beginning of rnd and sl st into first bsc (120 sts).

Rnd 20: Ch 1, bsc into same st, *sc into each of the next 19 sts, (sc, bsc) into the next st, rep from * around, ending with sc in same st as beginning of rnd and sl st into first bsc (126 sts).

Rnd 21: Ch 1, bsc into same st, *sc into each of the next 20 sts, (sc, bsc) into the next st, rep from * around, ending with sc in same st as beginning of rnd and sl st into first bsc (132 sts).

Rnd 22: Ch 1, bsc into same st, *sc into each of the next 21 sts, (sc, bsc) into the next st, rep from * around, ending with sc in same st as beginning of rnd and sl st into first bsc (138 sts).

Rnd 23: Ch 1, bsc into same st, *sc into each of the next 22 sts, (sc, bsc) into the next st, rep from * around, ending with sc in same st as beginning of rnd and sl st into first bsc (144 sts).

Rnd 24: Ch 1, bsc into the same st, *sc into each of the next 23 sts, bsc into the next st, rep from * around, ending with sl st into first bsc (144 sts).

Rnds 25–33: Rep rnd 24.

Rnd 34: Ch 1, *work bsc dec as follows: (insert hook in next st, yo and pull up a lp) twice, yo pull through all 3 lps on hook. Bsc dec made. Sc into each of next 22 sts, rep from * around. Join with sl st to first st (138 sts).

Rnd 35: Ch 1, *bsc dec once. Sc into each of next 21 sts, rep from * around. Join with sl st to first st (132 sts).

Rnd 36: Ch 1, *bsc dec once. Sc into each of next 20 sts, rep from * around. Join with sl st to first st (126 sts).

Rnd 37: Ch 1, *bsc dec once. Sc into each of next 19 sts, rep from * around. Join with sl st to first st (120 sts).

Rnd 38: Ch 1, *bsc dec once. Sc into each of next 18 sts, rep from * around. Join with sl st to first st (114 sts).

Rnd 39: Ch 1, *bsc dec once. Sc into each of next 17 sts, rep from * around. Join with sl st to first st (108 sts).

Rnd 40: Ch 1, *bsc dec once. Sc into each of next 16 sts, rep from * around. Join with sl st to first st (102 sts).

Rnd 41: Ch 1, *bsc dec once. Sc into each of next 15 sts, rep from * around. Join with sl st to first st (96 sts). At end of rnd 41, turn.

Rnds 42–45: Ch 1, sc in each st around. Join with a sl st to first sc of rnd. At end of rnd 45, fasten off yarn.

New skills/beaded increasing and decreasing in the round

Placing the beads where the increase and decrease happen makes a feature of the technique and also helps us remember where we have to increase or decrease. The technique is the same as normal, except we are placing a bead halfway through.

1 Work as normal to increase position.

2 Work first stitch of increase as normal, then place bead up at crochet hook, work single crochet into same place. Increase completed.

3 Work as normal to decrease position, then work first half of decrease as follows, insert hook into fabric, yo, and draw lp back through toward yourself (2 lps on hook).

4 Bring bead up to hook and finish off decrease by inserting hook into next stitch, yo and draw lp through toward yourself, yo again and draw through all lps on hook.

Project 12: Textured beaded bag

This bag is jam-packed full of different textures, colors, and stitches, and is a great way to test your crochet skills. The raw finish of the silk-and-cotton blend aran-weight yarns enhance the textural stitches. The glossy wooden beads add a little bit of fun, giving the bag a sugar-candy appearance.

before you start

MATERIALS

Yarn A: 2 x 50 g ball (1.75 oz) worsted-weight cotton and silk blend (approximately 118 yds/ 108 m per skein) in pink

Yarn B: 1 x 50 g ball (1.75 oz) worsted-weight cotton and silk blend (approximately 118 yds/ 108 m per skein) in cerise

Approximately 150 pink 8-mm wooden beads

HOOK SIZES

U.S. G-6 (4.5 mm) and U.S. H-8 (5.0 mm)

GAUGE/TENSION

13 sts and 10.5 rows to 4 in. (10 cm) over beaded pattern

FINISHED SIZE

12 in. (30 cm) wide by 11.5 in. (29 cm) tall

ABBREVIATIONS

bch—beaded chain

bpdc—back post double crochet

ch—chain

dc—double crochet

fpdc—front post double crochet

sc—single crochet

sk—skip

sl st—slip stitch

st—stitch(es)

BAG PANEL

Make 2.

Thread beads onto yarn A. Using yarn A and larger crochet hook, ch 38.

Row 1: Sc into second ch from hook and in each ch to end (37 sc). Ch 2, turn.

Row 2: Dc in each of the first 2 sts, * bch, sk one st, dc, repeat from * 16 more times, dc in the last st. Ch 1, turn.

Row 3: Sc into each sc and each ch space across (37 sc). Change to yarn B, ch 2, turn.

Row 4: Dc into each st across. Change to yarn A, ch 1, turn.

Row 5: Sc into each st across, ch 2, turn.

Rows 6–13: Repeat rows 2 through 5 twice more.

Rows 14–16: Repeat rows 2 through 4.

Row 17: Dc into each st across. Ch 2, turn.

Row 18–21: Dc in the first st. Alternate fpdc, bpdc across to form crochet rib pattern, ending dc into the turning chain.

HANDLE

Rows 22a–25a: Dc in the first st, *fpdc, bpdc, repeat from * 3 more times (9 dc in row), ch 2, turn. At end of row 25, skip final turning ch and finish off yarn.

Rows 22b–25b: Skipping 20 unworked sts from row 21, join with sl st in next dc. Ch 2, and work in fp/bp rib pattern for 4 rows to match right side. Do not break off yarn at end of row 25b. Instead, ch 20, skip unworked sts of row 21, and join with sl st in top of dc of row 25a. Sl st in remaining sts to end of row.

Row 26: Work first 9 sts of row, continuing in fp/bp rib pattern. Dc into each ch, and finish row in fp/bp rib pattern.

Rows 27–28: Dc in first st, *fpdc, bpdc, repeat from * across, ending dc in the last st. Finish off.

HANDLE TRIM

Using yarn B and smaller hook, join with sl st to bottom right hand corner of handle opening. Work 50 sc evenly around, joining in first sc of round with a sl st.

FINISHING OFF

Sew all loose ends into fabric. With wrong sides facing, stitch side and bottom seams together.

Project 13: Beaded necklace

This piece of jewelry is very simple to create, using basic increasing and decreasing techniques while working in the round. The ball and loop fastening at the back, the pewter beads worked into the joining chains, and the shimmer of the 4-ply lurex yarn all give this necklace a special feel.

before you start

MATERIALS
25 g (0.8 oz) lurex (approximately 104 yds/95 m per ball)
Approximately 100 small pewter glass beads
Small amount of polyester fiberfill

HOOK SIZE
U.S. steel size 4 (2 mm)

GAUGE/TENSION
Large bobble measures 1.25 in. (3 cm) in diameter

FINISHED SIZE
22 in. (56 cm) in length

ABBREVIATIONS
ch—chain
dec—decrease
lp(s)—loop(s)
rnd—round
sc—single crochet
sl st—slip stitch
st(s)—stitch(es)
yo—yarn over

LARGE BOBBLE
Make 1.

Ch 5, sl st in farthest ch from hook to form a ring.
Rnd 1: Ch 1, work 16 sc into ring. Sl st into first sc (16 sts).
Rnd 2: Ch 1, work 2 sc into each st, end with sl st into first sc of rnd (32 sts).
Rnds 3–6: Ch 1, sc into each st around, join with sl st into first st.
Rnds 7–8: Ch 1, work decrease (dec) as follows: (insert hook in next st, yo and draw up a lp) twice, yo, draw through all 3 lps on hook. Decrease made. Dec around, ending with sl st in first st (16 sts, then 8 sts). Finish off.

SMALL BOBBLE
Make 3.

Ch 5, sl st in farthest ch from hook to form a ring.
Rnd 1: Ch 1, work 12 sc into ring. Sl st into first sc (12 sts).
Rnd 2: Ch 1, work 2 sc into each st, end with sl st into first sc of rnd (24 sts).
Rnds 3–6: Ch 1, sc into each st around, join with sl st into first st.
Rnd 7: Ch 1, work decrease (dec) as follows: (insert hook in next st, yo and draw up a lp) twice, yo, draw through all 3 lps on hook. Decrease made. Dec around, ending with sl st in first st (12 sts). Finish off.

NECKLACE CHAIN
Thread all beads onto yarn. Ch 25, sl st in farthest ch from hook to make a ring.
Row 1: Ch 40,* bring 3 beads up to hook and work 1 ch as normal, ch 2, rep from * 11 more times. Sl st into top of first small bobble, ch 2, rep from * to * 12 times to match other side, ch 40, sl st into top of second small bobble. Break off.
Row 2: Rejoin yarn to top of large bobble with sl st. Ch 2, *bring 3 beads up to hook, ch 1 as normal, rep from * 4 more times. Sl st into bottom of third small bobble. Break off.
Row 3: Rejoin yarn to top of third small bobble with sl st. Ch 2, *bring 3 beads up to hook, ch 1 as normal, rep from * twice more and sl st into bottom of second small bobble (at center front of necklace). Finish off yarn.

New skills/inserting stuffing

To help the crochet ball keep its shape, it is best to insert some stuffing into the center before sewing up the opening at the top.

With the flat end of the crochet hook, poke a small amount of stuffing into the top opening of the ball. Keep doing this until the ball is quite firm.

2 Using the end of yarn at top opening or if sewn in attach another piece of the yarn and darn it in and out around the stitches at top opening.

3 Pull together to close the opening and sew in loose ends.

Project 14: Earflap hat

This hat can be worn in a variety of ways, so it's perfect for those changeable days. Worked on the round using a chunky tweedy yarn, the hat is given a bit of a twist with the woven-effect textured border.

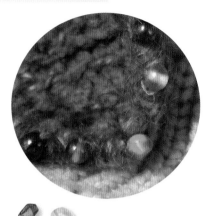

PATTERN

Using yarn A and larger hook, ch 4 and join together with a slip stitch to form a ring.

Rnd 1: Ch 1, 15 sc into ring. Join with sl st to first sc.

Rnd 2: Ch 1, (sc into next 2 sc, 2 sc into next sc) 5 times. Join with sl st to first sc (20 sts).

Rnd 3: Ch 1, (sc into next 3 sc, 2 sc into next sc) 5 times. Join with sl st to first sc (25 sts).

Rnd 4: Ch 1, (sc into next 4 sc, 2 sc into next sc) 5 times. Join with sl st to first sc (30 sts).

Rnd 5: Ch 1, sc into each st around. Join with sl st to first sc.

Rnd 6: Ch 1, (sc into next 5 sc, 2 sc into next sc) 5 times. Join with sl st to first sc (35 sts).

Rnds 7 and 8: Repeat rnd 5.

Rnd 9: Ch 1, (sc into next 6 sc, 2 sc into next sc) 5 times. Join with sl st to first sc (40 sts).

Rnds 10–14: Repeat rnd 5.

Rnds 15–21: Ch 1, sc into back loop only of each st around. Join with sl st to first sc. Break off yarn.

EARFLAPS

Using larger hook and yarn A, with wrong side of work facing, join with sl st 6 stitches from back seam.

Row 1: Ch 1, sc into front loop only of next 9 sts, turn.

Row 2: Ch 1, sc into back loop only of next 9 sts, turn.

before you start

MATERIALS

Yarn A: worsted-weight 100% wool (approximately 109 yds/100 m per 3.5 oz/100 g) in brown
Yarn B: aceweight kid-mohair-and-silk blend (approximately 225 yds/ 205 m per 0.8 oz/25 g) in lime
Yarn C: laceweight kid-mohair-and-silk blend (approximately 225 yds/ 205 m per 0.8 oz/25 g) in brown
Yarn D: laceweight kid-mohair-and-silk blend (approximately 225 yds/ 205 m per 0.8 oz/25 g) in turquoise
Yarn E: laceweight kid-mohair-and-silk blend (approximately 225 yds/ 205 m per 0.8 oz/25 g) in mint
Yarn F: laceweight kid-mohair-and-silk blend (approximately 225 yds/ 205 m per 0.8 oz/25 g) in khaki
Approximately 60 multicolored glass beads
2 large brown buttons

HOOK SIZE

U.S. L-11 (8.0 mm) and U.S. G-6 (4.0 mm)

GAUGE/TENSION

9 stitches and 11 rows per 4 in. (10 cm)

FINISHED SIZE

15.75 in. (40 cm) diameter, and 10 in. (25 cm) long

ABBREVIATIONS

bdc—beaded double crochet
beg—beginning
bsc—beaded single crochet
ch—chain
dec—decrease
sc—single crochet
sl st—slip stitch
st(s)—stitch(es)
yo—yarn over

Rows 3–10: Repeat earflap rows 1 and 2 four more times.

Row 11: Ch 1, working in front loops only, decrease (dec) as follows: *insert hook in front loop of next st and pull up a loop, repeat from * once, yo and pull through all 3 loops on hook. Dec made. Sc in front loops across to last 2 sts, work dec (7 sts).

Rows 12–13: Repeat earflap row 11. Break off yarn.

Skipping 11 sts on rnd 21 of hat, make second flap to match the first.

Sew in all loose ends.

TRIM

Using all kid-mohair-and-silk yarns together as one, thread beads onto yarn.

Using smaller hook and with wrong side facing, rejoin yarn at back seam.

Ch 1, bsc into first stitch at outer edge, (sc, bdc) evenly around the outer edge of hat and around earflaps. Join with sl st to beg ch 1.

Sew buttons into position on hat and pin back flaps.

Project 15: Beaded head band

This is the perfect solution to those bad hair days. Working in a DK cotton using a small hook gives the head band its stretch and ease. The circular crochet units are quick and easy to make. Finish with a sprinkling of beads or sequins.

before you start

MATERIALS
DK-weight cotton (approx 97 yds/ 89 m per 1.75 oz/50 g) in ecru
Approximately 100 4-mm black beads

HOOK SIZE
U.S. D-3 (3.25 mm)

GAUGE/TENSION
No real tension required

FINISHED SIZE
1.5 in. (3.8 cm) wide, 18 in. (45 cm) long unstretched

ABBREVIATIONS
ch—chain
dec—decrease
sc—single crochet
sl st—slip stitch
st(s)—stitch(es)
yo—yarn over

CIRCLES
Make 6.

Wrap the yarn approximately 10 times around 2 fingers on your left hand. Work a sc around the yarn to secure the ring. Work another 20–30 sc into the ring until you have filled the ring with sts. Sl st into the first sc of round. Fasten off.
Sew all six rings together to form a strip.

MAKING THE STRAP
Join with sl st to outer edge of ring opposite the rest of the strip.

Row 1: Work 5 sc along this edge, turn.
Row 2: Ch 1, sc into each sc across, turn (5 sts).

Row 3: Repeat row 2.
Row 4: Ch 1, decrease (dec) as follows: (insert hook in next st and pull up a loop) twice, yo, pull through all 3 lps on hook. Dec made. Sc once, dec over last 2 sts, turn (3 sts).
Row 5: Ch 1, sc in each of the 3 sts, turn.
Rows 6–25: Repeat row 5 another 20 times or until strap measures required length, keeping in mind that work will stretch in length.
Row 26: Ch 1, 2 sc into first st, sc into next stitch, 2 sc into last stitch, turn (5 sts).
Rows 27–29: Ch 1, sc in each of the 5 sts, turn.
Fasten off. Stitch into position at other side. Stitch beads into place along head band, according to photo.

Project 16: Brooch and pendant

These funky pieces are so easy to make; created from a simple crochet ball or loop, with beads sewn around the edges as decoration. The tweedy texture of the pure new wool 4-ply yarn used in the brooch, together with the mixed beads give the piece an organic feel. The pewter beads complement the shimmer of the 4-ply lurex yarn to make the necklace a special, sparkly little piece. Both pieces are so quick and easy to make that you'll soon be inspired to strike out and make your own design variants!

BROOCH

Ch 5, sl st in farthest ch from hook to form a ring.

Rnd 1: Ch 1, 9 sc into ring, sl st first sc (9 sts).
Rnd 2: Ch 1, 2 sc into each st around, sl st in first sc (18 sts).
Rnd 3: Ch 1, sc into each st, sl st in first sc.
Rnds 4–5: Repeat rnd 3.
Rnd 6: Ch 1, *decrease (dec) as follows: (insert hook in next st and pull up a loop) twice, yo, pull through all 3 loops on hook. Dec made. Repeat from * around. Sl st in first dec of round (9 sts).
Insert small amount of fiberfill into center of brooch and run yarn around top of opening. Draw up yarn to close. Fasten off. Sew beads into position using picture as a guide. Stitch pin finding into position at back.

before you start

BROOCH MATERIALS
Worsted-weight 100% wool (approximately 120 yds/110 m per 0.8 oz/25 g) in natural
Nine 8-mm glass beads in various colors
Nine 4-mm glass beads in orange
Polyester fiberfill
Pin jewelry finding

HOOK SIZE
U.S. steel size 8 (1.25 mm)

FINISHED SIZE
1.5 in. (4 cm) diameter including beads

ABBREVIATIONS
ch—chain
dec—decrease
rnd—round
sc—single crochet
sl st—slip stitch
st(s)—stitch(es)
yo—yarn over

PENDANT MATERIALS
Sport-weight 100% wool (approximately 123 yds/113 m per 0.8 oz/25 g) in teal
Twelve 8-mm beads
Approximately 60 4-mm beads
Polyester fiberfill
Approximately one yard/meter of leather cording

HOOK SIZE
U.S. B-1 (2.5 mm)

ABBREVIATIONS
ch—chain
dc—double crochet
sc—single crochet
sl st—slip stitch
st(s)—stitch(es)

PENDANT

Make 2 sides.

Ch 15, join with a sl st in farthest ch from hook to form a ring.

Rnd 1: Ch 1, 18 sc into ring, join with sl st into first sc (18 sts).

Rnd 2: Ch 1, 2 sc into each st around, sl st into first sc (36 sts).

Rnd 3: Sl st into the first 9 sts, sc in next 3 sts, dc in next 5 sts. 2 dc into each of the next 2 sts, dc in next 5 sts, sc in next 3 sts, sl st into last 9 sts. Fasten off yarn. Back stitch two discs together along outside edges. Stuff the disk with fiberfill and sew along inside edges. Sew beads onto bottom of pendant, using photo as guideline.

Use a lark's-head knot to loop cording through center of pendant.

Garments

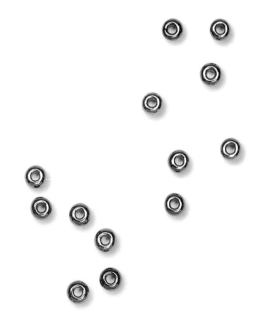

Project 17: Box crew-neck

This crochet edge-to-edge jacket is a great addition to your wardrobe. Worked in a DK-weight wool-and-cotton blend, the rounded appearance of the yarn brings a crispness to the stitch. This is a great way to progress onto garments and will help you understand how they are put together.

before you start

MATERIALS

Yarn A: 300 g (10.5 oz) DK-weight wool/ cotton blend (approximately 124 yds/113 m per 1.75 oz/50 g) in lavender

Yarn B: 50 g (1.75 oz) sport-weight merino wool (approximately 192 yds/175 m per 1.75 oz/50 g) in gray. Approximately 500 pewter gray 4-mm beads

HOOK SIZE

U.S. E-4 (3.5 mm)

GAUGE/TENSION

20 stitches and 9.5 rows to 4 in. (10 cm) over mesh pattern

FINISHED SIZE

17.75 in. (45 cm) long, 36 in. (90 cm) finished bust

ABBREVIATIONS

ch—chain
bch—beaded chain
bsc—beaded single crochet
dc—double crochet
rs—right side
sc—single crochet
sl st—slip stitch
sp(s)—space(s)
st(s)—stitch(es)
ws—wrong side
yo—yarn over

BACK PANEL

Make 1.

Using yarn A, ch 91.

Row 1: Dc into third ch from hook and each ch to end (89 dc incl turning ch).

Row 2: Ch 2, dc into first 2 dc, *ch 1, skip 1 st, dc into next st. Repeat from * across. Dc in turning ch. Turn (44 ch sps).

Rows 3–21: Ch 2, dc into next dc and next ch sp, *ch 1, skip dc, dc into next ch sp, repeat from * ending with dc in turning ch. Turn.

Shape raglan as follows:

Rows 22–41: Sl st across the first 4 sts, ch 3 (counts as dc), dc in next ch sp. *Ch 1, skip dc, dc into next ch sp, repeat from *

ending with dc in turning ch. Turn. At end of row 41, you should have 43 sts remaining. Fasten off yarn.

FRONT PANEL

Make 2.

Using yarn A, ch 44.

Row 1: Repeat row 1 of back panel (20 ch sps).

Rows 2–21: Repeat rows 2–21 of back panel.

Shape raglan as follows:

Row 22: Sl st across the first 2 sts, ch 3 (counts as dc), dc in next ch sp. *Ch 1, skip dc, dc into next ch sp, repeat from * ending with dc in turning ch. Turn.

Row 23: Ch 2, dc into next dc and next ch sp, *ch 1, skip dc, dc into next ch sp, repeat from * until one mesh remains. Dc in last ch sp, dc in next dc. Skip remaining 2 sts of row. Turn.

Rows 24–33: Repeat rows 22 and 23 another 5 times.

Row 34: Repeat row 22 once more. Shape neck as follows:

Row 35: Ch 2, double crochet decrease (dc dec) across next dc and ch sp as follows: (yo, insert hook in next st or sp, yo and pull up a loop, yo, pull through 2 loops) twice, yo, pull through all 3 loops on hook. Dc dec made. *Ch 1, skip dc, dc into next ch sp, repeat from * until one mesh remains. Dc in last ch sp, dc in next dc. Skip remaining 2 sts of row. Turn.

Row 36: Sl st across the first 2 sts, ch 3 (counts as dc), dc in next ch sp. *Ch 1, skip dc, dc into next ch sp, repeat from * until one ch sp remains. Dc dec across ch sp and next dc. Skip turning ch, turn.

Row 37: Repeat row 35.

Row 38: Repeat row 36.

Row 39: Repeat row 23.

Row 40: Repeat row 22.

Row 41: Repeat row 23.

SLEEVE

Make 2.

Using yarn A, ch 56.

Row 1: Dc into third ch from hook and each ch to end (54 dc).

Row 2: Ch 2, dc into first 2 dc, *ch 1, skip 1 st, dc into next st. Repeat from * across. Dc in turning ch. Turn (26 ch sps).

Row 3: Ch 2, dc into next dc and next ch sp, *ch 1, skip dc, dc into next ch sp, rep from * ending with dc in turning ch. Turn.

Row 4: Ch 2, dc into first 2 dc. *Ch 1, skip 1 st, dc into next st. Repeat from * across. Ch 1, work 2 dc in turning ch. Turn.

Rows 5–22: Repeat rows 3 and 4 another 9 times. At end of row 22, you should have 64 sts (31 ch sps).

Row 23: Sl st across the first 4 sts, ch 3 (counts as dc), dc in next ch sp. *Ch 1, skip dc, dc into next ch sp, repeat from * until two ch sps remain unworked. Skip rem. sts of row, turn (59 sts, 29 ch sps).

Row 24: Sl st across the first 2 sts, ch 3 (counts as dc), dc in next ch sp. *Ch 1, skip dc, dc into next ch sp, repeat from * until one ch sp remains unworked. Skip remaining sts of row, turn.

Rows 25–27: Repeat row 24.

Row 28: Sl st across the first 2 sts, ch 3 (counts as dc), dc in next ch sp. *Ch 1, skip dc, dc into next ch sp, rep from * across, turn. Repeat row 28 until 8 meshes remain. Finish off.

FINISHING

Sew shoulder seams, then set in sleeves. Sew side seams.

TRIM

Thread beads onto yarn B.

Rnd 1: With rs of work facing, work in unworked loops of front and back panels row 1 foundation chain. Join with sl st to bottom inside corner of left front. Ch 1, sc in each st along lower edge. Work 3 sts in the corner. Continue up side of front to neck edge. Work 3 sc in the corner. Continue working sc evenly along neck edge, placing 3 sc in each corner around entire garment. Sl st to first sc to join. Even though you are working in rounds, turn.

Rnd 2: Ch 1, sc in each st of previous round, working 3 sts into each corner until you reach the lower left front corner. Across the bottom edge of garment, make *5 bch, skip 2 sc, sc in the next st. Repeat from * across to end. Sl st into first sc of round 2.

SLEEVE TRIM

Thread beads onto yarn B.

Rnd 1: With ws facing, work in unworked loops of sleeve row 1 foundation chain. Join with sl st along side seam. Ch 1, sc in each st around. Join with sl st to first sc of rnd. Do not turn.

Rnd 2: Ch 1, *ch 5, skip 2 sc, sc in next st. Repeat from * around, ending sl st in first bsc of rnd. Fasten off.

Project 18: Slash-neck vest

This top looks far more complicated than it actually is. Worked in an open lace pattern, using an aran-weight cotton-and-silk blend, you will see results very quickly working through basic shaping techniques on the body. The beaded tie-belt feature is worked separately and then sewn on to the body.

before you start

MATERIALS

4 (5,5) 50 g (1.75 oz) balls of cotton-and-silk blend (approximately 127 yds/ 116 m per hank) in red
Approximately 75 purple 6-mm beads

HOOK SIZE

U.S. J-10 (6.0 mm)

GAUGE/TENSION

One 12-stitch pattern repeat and 6 rows to 3.5 in. (9 cm)

ABBREVIATIONS

bsc—beaded single crochet
ch—chain
dc—double crochet
rs—right side
sc—single crochet
sl st—slip stitch
sp(s)—space(s)
st(s)—stitch(es)
tr—treble crochet
ws—wrong side

FINISHED SIZE

Small: 28 inch (71 cm) finished bust, 22.5 in. (57 cm) long
Medium: 35 inch (89 cm) finished bust, 26 in. (66 cm) long
Large: 42 inch (107 cm) finished bust, 29.5 in. (75 cm) long
Changes for each size S (M, L) are noted in parentheses.

PANEL
Make 2.

Ch 59 (62, 74).
Row 1: Sc into second ch from hook, (ch 5, skip 3 ch, sc in next ch) across. Ch 2, dc into last ch.
Row 2: Ch 1, sc into dc, skip ch 2 sp, * 7 dc into next ch 5 sp, sc into next ch 5 sp, ch 5, sc into next ch 5 sp, repeat from * across, ch 2, tr into last sc. Turn.
Row 3: Ch 1, sc into tr, *ch 5, sc into second dc of 7-dc group, ch 5, sc into sixth dc of same group, sc in next ch 5 sp, ** ch 5, sc into next ch 5 sp, repeat from * end repeat at **, ch 2, tr into last sc. Turn.
Repeat rows 2 and 3 an additional 9 (11, 13) times, then row 2 once more.
Shape arm hole.
Row 23 (27, 31): Ch 1, dc into sc, ch 3, sl st into next 2 dc, ch 1, sc into second dc of 7-dc group, ch 5, sc into 6th dc of same group, sc in ch 5 sp, ch 5, sc in next ch 5 sp, *ch 5, sc into second dc of 7-dc group, ch 5, sc into 6th dc of same group, ch 5, sc into next ch 5 space, rep from * 2 (3, 4) times more. Ch 2, dc in last sc. Turn.

Row 24 (28, 32): Sl st into first 2 ch, sl st in sc, sl st in first 3 ch of ch 5 loop. Ch 3, 3 dc in same ch 5 loop, *sc into next ch 5 loop, ch 5, sc in next ch loop, 7 dc in next ch loop, sc in next loop, ch 5, repeat from * 1 (2, 3) times more, sc in next loop, 4 dc into last ch 5 loop. Turn.
Row 25 (29, 33): Ch 4, sc into third dc, *ch 5, sc into next ch loop, ch 5, sc into second dc of 7-dc group, ch 5, sc into 6th dc of same group, repeat from * 1 (2, 3) more times, ch 5, sc into second dc, ch 4, sc into turning ch. Turn.
Row 26 (30, 34): Ch 3, 3 dc in ch5 loop, *sc in next ch 5 loop, ch 5, sc in next loop, 7 dc in next ch loop, sc in next loop, ch 5, repeat from * across ending sc in next loop, 4 dc in last loop. Turn.
Repeat last 2 rows 5 (6, 7) more times.
Row 37 (43, 49): Ch 1, sc into first dc, ch 5, sc into ch 5 loop, ch 5, sc into fourth dc of 7-dc group, repeat from * across, ending ch 5, sc into last dc. Fasten off yarn.

BEADED TIE

Make 1.

Thread beads on yarn. Ch 8.

Row 1 (rs): Dc into third ch from hook and in each ch to end. Turn.

Row 2 (ws): Ch 1, * bsc across. Turn.

Row 3: Ch 2, sc into each st across. Turn.

Repeat Rows 2 and 3 another 4 times.

Work even in dc until strap measures approximately 48 (56, 64) in. or 123 (142, 166) cm, ending ready to work a ws row.

Repeat Rows 2 and 3 another 5 times.

Final Row: Ch 2, dc in each st across. Finish off.

ASSEMBLY

Sew body panels together along shoulder and side seams. Place marker at center of beaded tie, and match to side seam. Stitch tie into position along bottom of garment.

Project 19: Halter-neck top

This fresh, feminine top is perfect for hot summer days. Simple and sophisticated, the detailing is all at the back and fastenings. The vertical beaded shell trims and crochet chains zig-zag across the back. Worked in medium-weight cotton, this top will keep you cool.

before you start

MATERIALS

5 (6, 7) 50 g (1.75 oz) balls of sock weight cotton (approximately 124 yds/113 m per ball) in lilac
Approximately 300 purple beads
Approximately 300 blue beads

HOOK SIZE

U.S. E-4 (3.5 mm)

GAUGE/TENSION

18 sts and 12 rows to 4 in. (10 cm)

TO FIT BUST SIZES

32 (36, 40) in., [81 (91, 101) cm]

ABBREVIATIONS

bdc—beaded double crochet
bsc—beaded single crochet
ch—chain
dc—double crochet
dc dec—double crochet decrease
rs—right side
sc—single crochet
sl st—slip stitch
sp—space
st(s)—stitch(es)
ws—wrong side
yo—yarn over

BODICE FRONT

Make 1. Note that instructions are written for smallest size, with changes in stitch count for sizes medium and large indicated in parentheses as follows: S (M, L). If only one st count is given, it applies to all sizes. Ch 78 (90, 102).

Row 1: Sc into second ch from hook and each ch to end, turn. 77 (89, 101) sts.

Row 2: Ch 3, dc in each st across, turn.

Rows 3 and 4: Repeat row 2.

Sizes M and L ONLY: Repeat row 2 one more time. Resume instructions at row 5 below.

Row 5: Ch 3 (counts as dc), double crochet decrease (dc dec) as follows: (yo, insert hook into next st and pull up a loop, yo pull through 2 loops) twice, yo and draw through all 3 loops on hook. Dc dec made. Dc in each st across until 3 sts remain. Dc dec over next 2 sts, dc in last st, turn. [75 (87, 99) sts]

Row 6: Ch 3 (counts as dc), dc in each st across, turn.

Row 7: Repeat row 5 [73 (85, 97) sts].

Row 8: Repeat row 6.

Row 9: Repeat row 5 [71 (83, 95) sts].

Row 10: Repeat row 5 [69 (81, 93) sts].

Row 11: Repeat row 5 [67 (79, 91) sts].

Row 12: Repeat row 6.

Row 13: Repeat row 5 [65 (77, 89) sts].

Row 14: Repeat row 6.

Row 15: Repeat row 5 [63 (75, 87) sts].

Rows 16–17: Repeat row 6 twice.

Size M and L ONLY: Repeat row 6 a third time. Resume instructions at row 18 below.

Row 18: Ch 3, dc in the first st, 2 dc in the next st, dc in each st across until 2 sts remain, 2 dc in the next st, dc in the last st, turn [65 (77, 89) sts].

Row 19: Repeat row 6.

Row 20: Repeat row 18 [67 (79, 91) sts].

Row 21: Repeat row 6.

Row 22: Repeat row 18 [69 (81, 93) sts].

Row 23: Repeat row 6.

Row 24: Repeat row 18 [71 (83, 95) sts].

Row 25: Repeat row 6.

Row 26: Repeat row 18 [73 (85, 97) sts].

Row 27: Repeat row 6.

Row 28: Repeat row 18 [75 (87, 99) sts].

Row 29: Repeat row 6.

Row 30: Repeat row 18 [77 (89, 101) sts].

Sizes M and L ONLY: Repeat row 6 once. Resume instructions at row 31.

Row 31: Sl in first 8 (10, 12) sts of row. Ch 1, sc in next 61 (74, 87) sts, turn.

Row 32: Ch 3 (counts as first dc), 2 dc in each of the next 2 sts, dc across until 3 sts remain, 2 dc in each of the next 2 sts, dc in the last st, turn [65 (78, 91) sts].

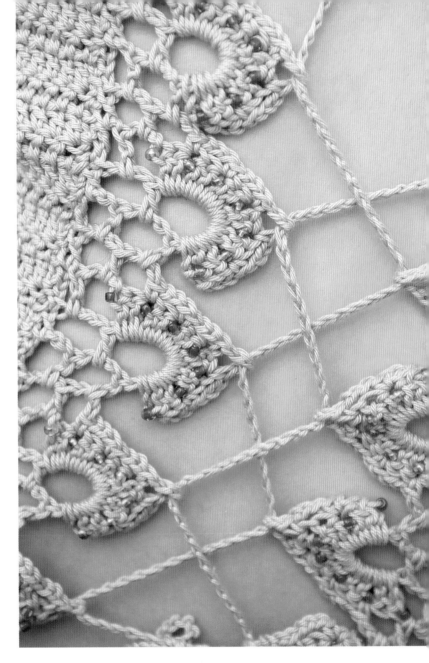

Rows 33–34: Repeat row 6 twice.

Rows 35–47 (49, 51): Repeat row 5 until 43 (52, 61) sts remain. Finish off.

BODICE BACK PANELS

Make 2.

Ch 29 (32, 35).

Row 1: Sc into second ch from hook and each ch to end, turn. 28 (31, 34) sts.

Row 2: Ch 3, dc in each st across, turn.

Rows 3 and 4: Repeat row 2.

Sizes M and L ONLY: Repeat row 2 one more time. Resume instructions at row 5.

Row 5: Ch 3 (counts as dc), dc dec. Dc in each st across, turn. [27 (30, 33) sts]

Row 6: Ch 3 (counts as dc), dc in each st across, turn.

Row 7: Repeat row 5 [26 (29, 32) sts].

Row 8: Repeat row 6.

Row 9: Repeat row 5 [25 (28, 31) sts].

Row 10: Repeat row 5 [24 (27, 30) sts].

Row 11: Repeat row 5 [23 (26, 29) sts].

Row 12: Repeat row 6.

Row 13: Repeat row 5 [22 (25, 28) sts].

Row 14: Repeat row 6.

Row 15: Repeat row 5 [21 (24, 27) sts].

Rows 16–17: Repeat row 6 twice.

Sizes M and L ONLY: Repeat row 6 a third time. Resume instructions at row 18 below.

Row 18: Ch 3, dc in the first st, 2 dc in the next st, dc in each st across, turn [22 (25, 28) sts].

Row 19: Repeat row 6.

Row 20: Repeat row 18 [23 (26, 29) sts].

Row 21: Repeat row 6.

Row 22: Repeat row 18 [24 (27, 30) sts].

Row 23: Repeat row 6.

Row 24: Repeat row 18 [25 (28, 31) sts].

Row 25: Repeat row 6.

Row 26: Repeat row 18 [26 (29, 32) sts].

Row 27: Repeat row 6.

Row 28: Repeat row 18 [27 (30, 33) sts].

Row 29: Repeat row 6.

Row 30: Repeat row 18 [28 (31, 34) sts].

Sizes M and L ONLY: Repeat row 6 once.

ALL SIZES: Fasten off.

BODICE CENTER BACK PANELS

Make 2.

Thread beads onto yarn in the following sequence: *7 purple, 7 blue, repeat from *, until you have 79 (84, 84) beads threaded.

Row 1: Ch 11, dc in seventh ch from hook, ch 3, skip 3 ch, dc in last ch, turn.

Row 2: Ch 7, skip dc, dc in ch 3 sp, ch 3, skip dc, dc in ch 6 sp, turn.

Row 3: Ch 5, skip dc, dc in ch 3 sp, ch 3, skip dc, (bdc, dc) 6 times in ch 7 sp, bdc in same sp, turn.

Row 4: Ch 3, skip first bdc and dc, (sc in next dc, ch 3, skip next dc) 5 times, sc into next dc, ch 3, dc in ch 3 sp, ch 3, dc in ch 5 sp, turn.

Row 5: Ch 5, skip first dc, dc in ch 3 sp, ch 3, dc in next ch 3 sp, turn.

Repeat rows 2 through 5 another 4 (5, 5) times. Fasten off.

ASSEMBLY

Sew front bodice to side panels along side seams. Sew center back panels to back bodice panels.

HALTER TOP EDGING.

Thread remaining beads onto yarn, alternating purple and blue throughout. With ws facing, join with sl st at upper corner of back bodice panel. Ch 1, bsc in every st along straight edge. Then working up side of sloped edge, work 2 bsc around each dc, ending with one bsc in upper corner. Work a long chain for neck strap, skip sts along the upper row of bodice. Begin bsc again in next corner and work down sloped side, working 2 bsc in the end of each row, then bsc in each dc along top of remaining back bodice panel. Finish off.

DIAGRAM OF BEADED HALTER TOP

Body measurements sizes: small 32" bust • medium 36" bust • large 40" bust

1 square = 1 row or 1 stitch

4.5 sts/inch 3dc rows/inch

75 sts wide = 16.6"—33" finished bust (27" waist) • 37" finished bust (31" waist) • 41" finished bust (35" waist)

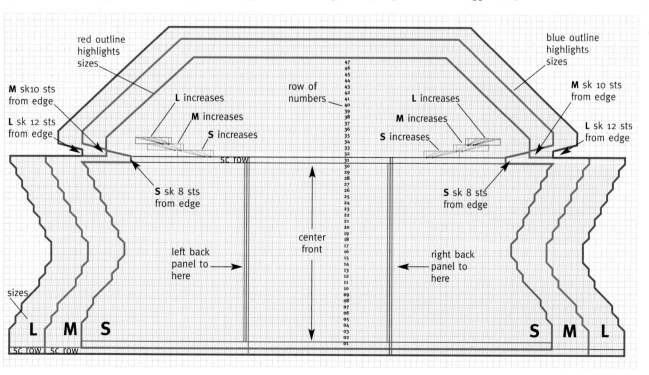

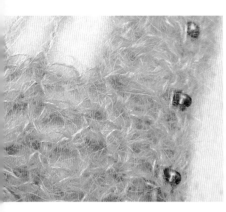

Project 20: Cobweb shrug

The shrug has become a new modern essential and can be found in lots of different shapes and sizes. In this design, each square is worked separately then stitched together to form the body and sleeves in one. The soft 2-ply yarn makes it ideal for summer evenings or layering up for winter nights. The beaded trim adds weight to the cobweb-light fabric.

before you start

MATERIALS

3 x 25 g (0.8 oz) laceweight kid-mohair-and-silk blend (approximately 230 yds/210 m per ball) in turquoise
Approximately 250 purple glass beads

HOOK SIZE

U.S. E-4 (3.5 mm)

GAUGE/TENSION

Each motif 5 in. (12 cm) square

FINISHED SIZE

25 in. (63 cm) cuff to cuff and 15 in. (38 cm) long

ABBREVIATIONS

bsc—beaded single crochet
ch—chain
dc—double crochet
rep—repeat
rnd—round
sc—single crochet
sl st—slip stitch
sp(s)—space(s)
st(s)—stitch(es)
ws—wrong side

MOTIF

Make 21.

Ch 10, join with sl st to form a ring.

Row 1: Ch 13, (work 5 dc into ring, ch 11) 3 times, 3 dc into ring, sl st to third ch of beginning ch 13.

Row 2: Sl st into each of the next 5 ch, ch 3 (counts as dc), (2 dc, ch 3, 3 dc) into same ch sp, * ch 9, (3 dc, ch 3, 3 dc) into next ch sp, rep from * twice more, ch 9, sl st to top of beginning ch 3.

Row 3: ch 3 dc into each of next 2 dc, *(3 dc, ch 3, 3 dc) into 3 ch sp, dc into each of next 3 dc, ch 4, skip 4 ch, sc into next ch, ch 3, sl st into base of last sc worked, ch 4, dc into each of next 3 dc, rep from * around. Sl st to top of beginning ch 3.

Fasten off yarn.

ASSEMBLY

Step 1: Sew together motifs 1 through 17 according to diagram below, leaving open those edges marked with thick orange lines.

Step 2: Connect a single edge of motifs 1 and 12 along dotted line. You should now have a circular strip of 12 motifs with an additional 5 motifs extending from one side.

Step 3: Sew motifs 14, 15, and 16 to the now-continuous edge of motifs 12, 1, and 2, as marked with thick yellow lines.

Step 4: Sew gusset motifs 18, 19, 20, and 21 in place along edges marked with thick orange lines.

DIAGRAM OF SHRUG

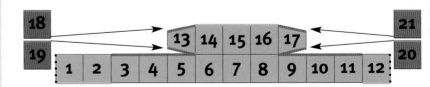

TRIM

Thread beads onto yarn. With ws facing, join with sl st along neck edge.

Rnd 1: Ch 1, sc into each st around the outer edge. Join with sl st into first ch.

Rnd 2: Ch 2, dc into each st around. Join with sl st into beginning ch 2.

Rnd 3: Ch 1, *sc in the next dc, bsc in the next dc, skip one dc, rep from * around. Join with sl st to first ch of rnd.

Project 21: Beaded tunic

Great for covering up at the beach or for throwing on over jeans. The chunky cotton yarn is worked in an open mesh fabric. The collar and front opening have a mandarin feel to them, edged with milky white pearlescent beads.

before you start

MATERIALS

Yarn A: twelve 50 g (1.75 oz) skeins worsted weight cotton (approximately 64 yds/58 m per ball) in pink
Yarn B: one 50 g (1.75 oz) skein DK-weight cotton (approximately 97 yds/89 m per ball) in pink
Approximately 400 white beads

HOOK SIZE

U.S. K-10.5 (7.0 mm) and U.S. G-6 (4.5 mm)

GAUGE/TENSION

13 stitches and 6 rows to 4 in. (10 cm).

FINISHED BUST SIZE

34 in. (86 cm), 23 in. (58 cm) in length

ABBREVIATIONS

beg—beginning
bsc—beaded single crochet
ch—chain
dc—double crochet
rem—remaining
rep—repeat
sc—single crochet
sl st—slip stitch
sp(s)—space(s)
st(s)—stitch(es)

TUNIC BACK

With yarn A and larger hook, ch 64.

Row 1: Dc into third ch from hook and each ch across. Turn (62 dc).
Row 2: Ch 2, dc into first 2 dc, *ch 1, skip 1 st, dc into next st. Rep from * across. Dc in turning ch. Turn (29 ch sps).
Rows 3–23: Ch 2, dc into next dc and next ch sp, *ch 1, skip dc, dc into next ch sp, rep from * ending with dc in turning ch. Turn (29 ch sps).

Shape for armholes as follows:
Row 24: Ch 1, sl st across 8 sts, ch 2, dc in same dc and in next ch sp, *ch 1, skip dc, dc into next ch sp, rep from * until 10 sts rem unworked, dc in next dc and in next ch sp. Turn (48 sts, 22 ch sps).
Rows 25–34: Ch 2, dc in first 2 sts, *ch 1, skip dc, dc into next ch sp, rep from * until 2 sts rem, dc in each of the last 2 sts, turn. At end of row 34, finish off.

TUNIC FRONT

Work rows 1 through 21 as for tunic back. Divide for upper front:
Rows 22A and 23A: Ch 2, 2 dc, (ch 1, dc in ch sp) 9 times. Dc in last dc, turn (22 sts, 9 ch sps).
Shape armholes:
Row 24A: Ch 1, sl st across 8 sts, ch 2, dc in same dc and in next ch sp, *ch 1, skip dc, dc into next ch sp, rep from * until 2 sts rem, dc in each of the last 2 dc. Turn (14 sts, 5 ch sps).

Rows 25A–34A: Ch 2, 2 dc, dc into ch sp, *ch 1, skip dc, dc into next ch sp, rep from * until 2 sts rem. Dc in last 2 sts, turn. Finish off.

For upper-right front
Row 22B: With rs facing, in unworked sts of row 21, skip 4 ch sps from left front and join yarn A with sl st in next dc. Ch 2, dc in ch sp, (ch 1, dc in ch sp) 12 times. Dc in last 2 sts (27 sts, 12 ch sps).
Row 23B: Ch 2, dc into next 2 dc and next ch sp, *ch 1, skip dc, dc into next ch sp, rep from * across. Dc in last 2 sts. Turn.
Row 24B: Ch 2, dc in next dc, (ch 1, skip dc, dc in ch sp) 8 times, dc in next dc. Leave rem 8 sts of row unworked for armhole. Turn (18 sts, 8 ch sps).

Row 25B: Ch 2, dc in next dc and in ch sp, (ch 1, skip dc, dc in ch sp) 7 times, dc in last 2 sts. Turn.
Row 26B: Ch 2, dc in next dc, (ch 1, skip dc, dc in ch sp) 7 times, ch 1, skip dc, dc in each of the last 2 sts.
Rows 27B–34B: Rep rows 25B and 26B four more times.

Finish off.

Make 2.

ASSEMBLY

Weave in all ends. Sew front to back at shoulder seams. Sew sleeve seams. Sew side seams.

NECK TRIM

Thread approximately 75 beads onto yarn B.

Using smaller hook, with right side of work facing, join yarn B with sl st to bottom edge of neck opening.

Row 1: Work 34 sc evenly up right front edge to neckline. Turn.

Row 2: Ch 1, bsc into each sc. Turn.

Row 3: Ch 1, sc into each bsc. Turn.

Repeat rows 2 and 3 once more.

Break off yarn.

Repeat these 5 rows for left front edge, beg from upper left neckline and working 34 sc evenly down the left front opening.

COLLAR TRIM

Thread 150 beads onto yarn B.

Using yarn B and smaller hook, with right side of work facing, join yarn to right front at top edge of neck trim and work along the neck edge.

Row 1: Ch 1, sc into the end of each of the 5 neck trim rows, sc in each sc and in each ch sp around neck edge, 5 sc into left front neck trim.

Row 2: Ch 1, sc in the first st, bsc into each sc around until 1 st rem, sc in the last st. Turn.

Row 3: Ch 1, sc into each st across. Turn.

Repeat rows 2 and 3 once more.

Finish off.

Weave in all ends. Block to finished size.

SLEEVES

Make 2.

Using yarn A and larger hook, ch 42.

Row 1: Dc into third ch from hook and each ch across. Turn (40 dc).

Row 2: Ch 2, dc into first 2 dc, *ch 1, skip 1 st, dc into next st. Repeat from * across. Dc in turning ch. Turn (40 sts, 18 ch sps).

Row 3: Ch 2, dc in the same sp, (ch 1, skip next dc, dc in the ch sp) across until 2 sts rem, 2 dc into next dc, dc in the turning ch. Turn (42 sts).

Row 4: Ch 2, dc in the same st, dc in the next st, (ch 1, skip next dc, dc in the ch sp) across, ending dc in each of the last 2 sts. Turn.

Row 5: Repeat row 4.

Row 6: Ch 2, dc in the same st, dc in the next st, (ch 1, skip next dc, dc in next ch sp) across, ending with dc in next dc, 2 dc in the turning ch. Turn (44 sts).

Row 7: Ch 2, dc in next st and in ch sp, (ch 1, skip dc, dc in ch sp) across, ending dc in each of the last 2 dc. Turn.

Row 8: Repeat row 7.

Row 9: Repeat row 3 (46 sts).

Row 10: Repeat row 4.

Row 11: Repeat row 4.

Row 12: Repeat row 6 (48 sts).

Row 13: Repeat row 7.

Row 14: Repeat row 7.

Row 15: Repeat row 3 (50 sts).

Rows 16–21: Repeat row 4.

Finish off.

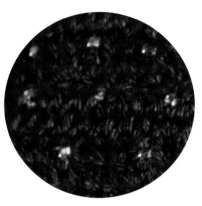

Project 22: Bikini top

This beaded bikini top is great for those hot sunny days. The turquoise glass beads scattered throughout almost seem to glow against the dark indigo background. The more you wear and wash this top, the more it will fade, just like your jeans, and become a firm favorite.

before you start

MATERIALS

2 x 50g (1.75 oz) DK-weight cotton (approximately 97 yds/89 m per ball) in dark indigo
Approximately 350 (425, 500) turquoise glass beads

HOOK SIZE

U.S. E-4 (3.5 mm)

GAUGE/TENSION

18 sts and 10 rows to 4 in. (10 cm)

FINISHED SIZES

To fit cup sizes A (B, C). Linear bust measurement is adjustable to any fit.

ABBREVIATIONS

bdc—beaded double crochet
bsc—beaded single crochet
ch—chain
dc—double crochet
dc dec—double crochet decrease
rep—repeat
rs—right side
sc—single crochet
sl st—slip stitch
st(s)—stitch(es)
yo—yarn over

BIKINI CUP

Make 2.
Note that instructions are written for cup size A, with changes in stitch count for cup sizes B and C indicated in parentheses as follows: [A (B, C)]. If only one st count is given, it applies to all sizes.
Thread half of beads onto yarn. Ch 36 (42, 48).

Row 1: Sc into second ch from hook, *bsc in next ch, sc in next ch, rep from * to end, turn. [35 (41, 47) sts]

Row 2: Ch 4, (counts as first dc plus ch 1), *skip sc, dc in bsc, ch 1, rep from * across, turn. [17 (20, 23) spaces].

Row 3: Ch 1, sc in first dc, *bsc in ch sp, sc in dc, rep from * across, turn [35 (41, 47) sts].

Row 4: Ch 2, dc in first st, work dc decrease (dc dec) as follows: *yo, insert hook in st, yo, pull up a loop, yo, draw through 2 loops, rep from * once more, yo, draw through all 3 loops on hook. Dc dec made. Rep dc dec over next 2 sts, dc in each st across row until last 3 sts of row remain, while evenly distributing 7 beads across row. Dc dec, then dc in last st, turn. [31 (37, 43) sts]

Size B ONLY: Rep row 4 once more, distributing 8 beads across row. Resume from row 5 below.

Size C ONLY: Repeat row 4 twice more, distributing 8 beads across row on first rep and 7 beads on the second rep. [31 (33, 35) sts]. Resume from row 5 below.

Row 5: Ch 2, dc in the first st, dc dec, dc in each st across until last 3 sts of row remain, distributing 6 beads across row. Dc dec, dc in the last st [29 (31, 33) sts].

Size B ONLY: Rep row 5 once more, distributing 7 beads across row. Resume from row 6 below.

Size C ONLY: Rep row 5 twice more, distributing 7 beads across row on first rep and 8 beads on the second rep. [29 (29, 29) sts]. Resume from row 6 below.

Row 6: Ch 2, dc in the first st, dc dec, dc in each st across until 3 sts remain, distributing 7 beads across row. Dc dec, dc [27 sts].

Row 7: Ch 2, dc in the first st, dc dec, dc in each st across until 3 sts remain, distributing 6 beads across row. Dc dec, dc [25 sts].

Row 8: Ch 2, dc in the first st, dc dec, dc in each st across until 3 sts remain, distributing 5 beads across row. Dc dec, dc [23 sts].

Row 9: Ch 2, dc in the first st, dc dec, dc in each st across until 3 sts remain, distributing 4 beads across row. Dc dec, dc [21 sts].

Row 10: Ch 2, dc in the first st, dc dec, dc in each st across until 3 sts remain, distributing 5 beads across row. Dc dec, dc [19 sts].

Row 11: Ch 2, dc in the first st, dc dec, dc in each st across until 3 sts remain, distributing 4 beads across row. Dc dec, dc [17 sts].

Row 12: Ch 2, dc in the first st, dc dec, dc in each st across until 3 sts remain, distributing 3 beads across row. Dc dec, dc [15 sts].

Row 13: Ch 2, dc in the first st, dc dec, dc in each st across until 3 sts remain, distributing 2 beads across row. Dc dec, dc [13 sts].

Row 14: Ch 2, dc in the first st, dc dec, dc in each st across until 3 sts remain, distributing 3 beads across row. Dc dec, dc [11 sts].

Row 15: Ch 2, dc in the first st, dc dec, dc in each st across until 3 sts remain, distributing 2 beads across row. Dc dec, dc [9 sts].

Row 16: Ch 2, dc in the first st, dc dec, dc, bdc, dc, dc dec, dc [7 sts].

Row 17: Ch 2, dc in the first st, dc dec, dc, dc dec, dc [5 sts].

Row 18: Ch 2, dc in the first st, (yo, insert hook in next st, yo and pull up loop, yo, pull through 2 loops on hook) three times, yo, and pull through all 4 loops on hook, dc in the last st [3 sts]. Finish off.

CUP BORDER

Thread beads onto yarn.

Row 1: With rs facing, join with sl st in lower right corner. (If working left-handed, join in lower left corner.) Ch 1, work approximately 60 sc evenly around 2 sides of cup, placing 3 sc in top corner, turn.

Row 2: Ch 1, bsc in first sc, *sc, bsc, rep from * across, working 3 sts in corner, turn.

Row 3: Ch 1, sc in each st, working 3 sts into corner, turn.

Row 4: Rep border row 2. Finish off.

NECK TIE

Join with sl st in corner st at top of cup border. *Ch 1, sc in next 2 sts, turn. Rep from * until tie measures 18 in. (45 cm) or desired length. Finish off.

Make second cup with border and neck tie identical to previous.

BODICE TIE

Make 1.

Ch 3, sc in second and farthest chs from hook. *ch 1, turn, sc in both sts, rep from * until tie measures approximately 48 in. (120 cm) or desired length. Finish off. Thread bodice tie through eyelets created in cup rows 2.

ASSEMBLY

Wash finished bikini top in hot water to remove excess indigo dye. Lay flat to dry.

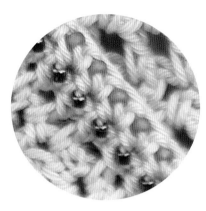

Project 23: Cap-sleeved wrap

Crocheted in a medium-weight 100% cotton yarn and worked in an open-mesh fabric with capped sleeves, this garment is light enough to fit under a jacket and is also great for wearing on its own on a summer day.

before you start

MATERIALS

300 g (10.5 oz) sport-weight cotton (approximately 124 yds/113 m per 1.75 ozs./50 g) in beige
Approximately 300 pewter 4-mm beads
Approximately 300 orange 4-mm beads

HOOK SIZE

U.S. G-6 (4.5 mm) and U.S. D-3 (3.25 mm)

GAUGE/TENSION

22 sts and 9.5 rows to 4 in. (10 cm) across mesh pattern

FINISHED SIZE

17.25 in. (43 cm) long, 32 in. (80 cm) finished bust

ABBREVIATIONS

bch—beaded chain.
bdc—beaded double crochet
bsc—beaded single crochet
ch—chain
dc—double crochet
lp(s)—loop(s)
rep—repeat
sc—single crochet
sl st—slip stitch
sp(s)—space(s)
st(s)—stitch(es)
yo—yarn over

BACK PANEL
With larger hook, ch 84.

Row 1: Dc into third ch from hook and each ch across. Turn (82 dc).
Row 2: Ch 2, dc into first 2 dc, *ch 1, skip 1 st, dc into next st. Rep from * across. Dc in turning ch. Turn (39 ch sps).
Rows 3–26: Ch 2, dc into next dc and next ch sp, *ch 1, skip dc, dc into next ch sp, rep from * ending with dc in turning ch. Turn (39 ch sps).

Shape armholes as follows:
Row 27: Sl st into first 2 dc and ch sp, ch 2, dc in next dc and ch sp. *Ch 1, skip dc, dc into next ch sp, rep from * ending with dc in turning ch. Turn (37 ch sps).
Rows 28–43: Rep row 3. Fasten off.

FRONT PANEL
Make 2.

With larger hook, ch 62.

Row 1: Dc into third ch from hook and each ch across. Turn (60 dc).
Row 2: Ch 2, dc into first 2 dc, *ch 1, skip 1 st, dc into next st. Rep from * across. Dc in turning ch. Turn (28 ch sps).
Rows 3–9: Ch 2, dc into next dc and next ch sp, *ch 1, skip dc, dc into next ch sp, rep from * ending with dc in turning ch. Turn (28 ch sps).
Shape neck edge as follows:
Row 10: Ch 2, work double crochet decrease (dc dec) as follows: (yo, insert

hook in next st or sp, yo and pull up a lp, yo, pull through 2 lps) twice, yo, pull through all 3 lps on hook. Dc dec made. *Ch 1, skip dc, dc into next ch sp, rep from * ending with dc in turning ch. Turn (27 ch sps).
Row 11: Ch 2, dc into next dc and next ch sp, *ch 1, skip dc, dc into next ch sp, rep from * ending with dc in top of dc dec. Turn (27 ch sps).
Rows 12–25: Rep rows 10 and 11 another 8 times until 19 ch sps remain.
Row 26: Rep row 10 once more.
Shape armhole as follows:
Row 27: Sl st into first 2 dc and ch sp, ch 2, dc in next dc and ch sp. *Ch 1, skip dc, dc into next ch sp, rep from *

ending with dc in turning ch. Turn (17 ch sps).
Rows 28–43: Rep rows 10 and 11 until 9 ch sps remain. Fasten off.

SLEEVE
Make 2.

Thread 68 pewter beads then 68 orange beads onto yarn. (The first bead threaded will be the last bead worked.)
Row 1: With larger hook, bch 68, then ch 2. Bdc into third ch from hook (this is bch nearest to hook) and in each bch to end, turn (68 bdc).

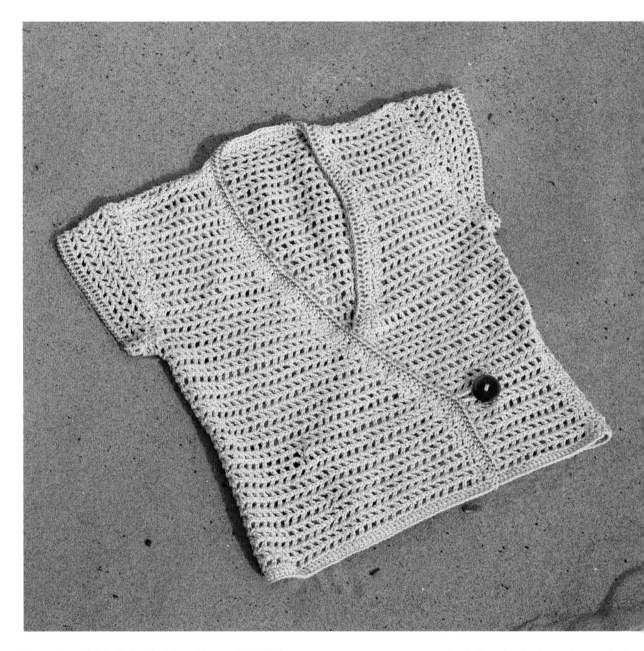

Row 2: Ch 2, dc into first 2 dc, *ch 1, skip 1 st, dc into next st. Rep from * across. Dc in turning ch. Turn (32 ch sps).

Row 3: Ch 1, sl st in first 4 sts, ch 2 (counts as dc), dc into next dc and next ch sp, *ch 1, skip dc, dc into next ch sp, rep from * across until 2 ch sps remain. Dc in next dc, sk remaining sts, turn (29 ch sps).

Rows 4–7: Rep row 3 until 17 ch sps remain. Fasten off yarn.

ASSEMBLY

Sew front panels to back at shoulder seams. Set in sleeves. Sew side seams.

TRIM

Thread 180 pewter beads then 180 orange beads onto yarn.

With ws facing, and using smaller hook, join with sl st to lower inside edge of left front. Ch 1, dc 183 sts evenly around edge, working 79 up left front, 25 across back neck, and 79 down right front. Turn.

Row 2: Ch 1, bsc into each dc of previous row. Break off yarn.

Row 3: Rejoin yarn with sl st to first bsc of Row 2. Ch 1, bsc into each st across. Fasten off.

FINISHING

Lay garment flat with right side facing. Stitch larger button into position on left hand side of cardigan. Place marker on right hand side trim and make 15 ch lp.

Turn the garment inside out and rep above process using smaller button and working 10 ch lp.

Block to required size.

New skills/Making a button loop

Button loops are very quick and easy to make, they can be made separately and stitched into position or worked into the fabric as given below. They are made up of a crochet chain with the ends stitched together side by side.

1 Using yarn and hook as given in pattern, rejoin the yarn to position required.

2 Make chain to required length, ensuring it will fit round the button being used. Remember that the lp will stretch slightly so make it on the small side.

3 Fasten off yarn and stitch end into the wrong side of garment next to where chain started.

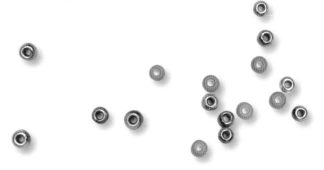

Project 24: Motifs for sweaters

Inspired by plants and flowers, these motifs are a great way to use up all your odd bits of yarn. Have fun with various color combinations and beads. They are also a good exercise in color changing, and great for getting to know the various crochet stitches.

before you start

MATERIALS

Yarn A: 25 g (0.8 oz) sport-weight 100% wool (approximately 120 yds/110 m per ball) in ginger

Yarn B: 25 g (0.8 oz) laceweight kid-mohair-and-silk blend (approximately 230 yds/210 m per ball) in turquoise

Yarn C: 25 g (0.8 oz) sport-weight lurex (approximately 104 yds/95 m per ball) in silver

Yarn D: 25 g (0.8 oz) sport-weight 100% wool (approximately 120 yds/110 m per ball) in green

Yarn E: 25 g (0.8 oz) laceweight kid-mohair-and-silk blend (approximately 230 yds/210 m per ball) in lilac

Yarn F: 25 g (0.8 oz) laceweight kid-mohair-and-silk blend (approximately 230 yds/210 m per ball) in cerise

Yarn G: 25 g (0.8 oz) laceweight kid-mohair-and-silk blend (approximately 230 yds/210 m per ball) in lime

Yarn H: 25 g (0.8 oz) sport-weight lurex (approximately 104 yds/95 m per ball) in brown

Yarn I: 25 g (0.8 oz) sport-weight 100% wool (approximately 120 yds/110 m per ball) in ecru

Yarn J: 25 g (0.8 oz) sport-weight 100% wool (approximately 120 yds/110 m per ball) in turquoise

Yarn K: 25 g (0.8 oz) sport-weight lurex (approximately 104 yds/95 m per ball) in pink

Approximately 100 clear silver-lined 4-mm glass beads

Approximately 20 light blue 4-mm glass beads

HOOK SIZE

U.S. E-4 (3.5 mm)

ABBREVIATIONS

bch—beaded chain
bdc—beaded double crochet
beg—beginning
bsc—beaded single crochet
ch—chain
dc—double crochet
hdc—half double crochet
rep—repeat
rnd—round
rs—right side
sc—single crochet
sk—skip
sl st—slip stitch
sp(s)—space(s)
st(s)—stitch(es)
tr—treble crochet
ws—wrong side
yo—yarn over

MOTIF 1

GAUGE/TENSION

Round 1 measures 1 x 1.25 in.
(2.5 x 3.2 cm)

FINISHED SIZE

3.25 in. (8.2 cm) square

Thread 10 silver-lined clear beads onto yarn C, set aside.

Thread 16 silver-lined clear beads onto yarn E, set aside.

With yarn A, ch 6, sl st in farthest ch from hook to form a ring.

Rnd 1: Ch 1, 3 sc, 2 hdc, 2 dc, 3 tr, 2 dc, 2 hdc, 3 sc, sl st into first sc. Change to yarn B.

Rnd 2: Sl st in first 3 sts, 2 hdc, (2 dc into next st) 3 times, 3 tr into next st, (2 dc into next st) 3 times, 2 hdc, 3 sl st, sl st into first sl st of round. Change to pre-beaded yarn C.

Rnd 3: Sl st in first 2 sts, 4 sc, 5 bsc, 3 sc into next st, 5 bsc, 4 sc, 2 sl st, end with sl st into first sl st of round. Change to yarn D.

Rnd 4: Sl st in first 4 sts, 2 sc, (2 sc into next st) 3 times, (2 dc into next st) 4 times, 3 tr into next st, (2 dc into next st) 4 times, (2 sc into next st) 3 times, 2 sc, 4 sl st, end with sl st into first st of round. Break off yarn.

Rnd 5: With pre-beaded yarn E, join with sl st into first sc of Rnd 4. Ch 1, sc in same st, (ch 2, bch, ch 2, sk next st, sc) 3 times, (ch 1, bch, ch 1, sk next st, sc) 10 times, (ch 2, bch, ch 2, sk next st, sc) 3 times. Fasten off.

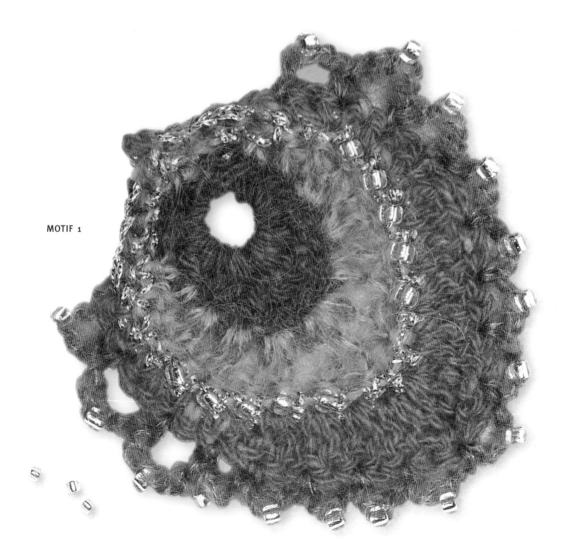

MOTIF 1

MOTIF 2

> **GAUGE/TENSION**
> Round 1 measures 2 x 0.5 in.
> (5 x 1.25 cm)
>
> **FINISHED SIZE**
> 3.25 x 1.5 in. (8.2 x 3.75 cm)

Thread 20 silver-lined clear beads onto yarn D and set aside.

Using yarn F, ch 13.
Row 1: Sc into second ch from hook, 3 hdc, 2 dc, 2 hdc, 4 sc. Do not turn (12 sts).
Rnd 2 (ws): Change to yarn A. Working in remaining lps of foundation ch, start next rnd at foundation ch and continue around last row. Ch 1, 11 sc, (sc, dc) into next st, (dc, sc) into next stitch, 11 sc, sc into ch at beg of rnd. Change to yarn G.

Rnd 2: Sl st in first sc, 2 sc, 2 hdc, 2 dc, 2 hdc, 4 sc, 2 dc into next st, 4 sc, 2 hdc, 2 dc, 2 hdc, 2 sc, 2 sl st. Sl st into first sl st of rnd. Change to pre-beaded yarn D.
Rnd 3: Sl st in first 5 sts, work 6 bsc, (bsc, 2 bdc) into next st, (bdc, bsc) into next st, 7 bsc, sl st in next 8 sts and in first sl st of rnd. Fasten off yarn.

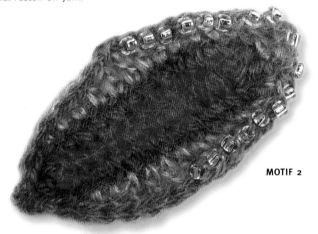

MOTIF 2

MOTIF 3

MOTIF 3

> **GAUGE/TENSION**
> Round 1 measures 0.375 in. (1 cm) across
>
> **FINISHED SIZE**
> 3.25 x 2.25 in. (8.2 x 5.6 cm)

Thread 16 silver-lined clear beads onto yarn E and set aside.
Thread 8 silver-lined clear beads onto yarn D and set aside.
Using yarn H, ch 6, sl st in farthest ch from hook to form a ring.
Row 1 (ws): Work 6 sc into ring. Do not join, turn. Change to yarn I.
Row 2 (rs): Ch 2, 2 dc, 2 dc into each of next 2 sts, 2 dc. Turn. Change to yarn F.

Row 3: Ch 2, 3 dc, 2 dc into each of next 2 sts, 3 dc. Turn. Change to beaded yarn E.
Row 4: Ch 2, 2 bdc into next st, 2 bdc, (2 bdc into next st) 4 times, 2 bdc, 2 bdc into next st. Turn. Change to pre-beaded yarn D.
Row 5: Ch 1, sc, (bsc, sc) 8 times. Sk last st, break off yarn.

Row 6: With rs facing, rejoin yarn C with sl st into beg ring. Work 8 sc along row edges, sc into top corner, *ch 5, sk 1 sc, sc, rep from * 7 times. Work 8 sc along row edges, sc into ring, sl st into first sc of round.

MOTIF 4

GAUGE/TENSION
Round 1 measures 0.75 in.
(1.8 cm) across

FINISHED SIZE
2.25 in. (5.6 cm) square

Thread 16 light blue beads onto yarn E
and set aside.

Using yarn K, ch 6, sl st in farthest ch
from hook to form a ring.
Rnd 1: Ch 1, 16 sc into ring, sl st into first
sc.
Rnd 2: Ch 1, sc into same st, sc into next
st, *(sc, ch 9, sc) into next st **, sc into
next 3 sts; rep from * twice, then from *
to ** once more. Sc into next st, sl st to
first sc.

Rnd 3: Ch 1, sc into same st, *skip 2 sc,
work [2 hdc, 17 dc, 2 hdc] into next ch 9
lp, sk next 2 sc, sc into next sc, rep from *
3 more times, omitting 1 sc at end of last
rep and sl st to first sc of round. Change
to pre-beaded yarn E.
Rnd 4: Ch 1, bsc over first st, *ch 5, sk 5
sts, sc into next st, ch 1, bch 1, ch 1, sl st

into sc just worked. (Ch 5, sk 4 sts, sc into
next st, ch 1, bch 1, ch 1, sl st into sc just
worked) twice. Ch 5, sk 5 sts, bsc over
next st, rep from * 3 times, omitting bsc at
end of last rep and sl st to first bsc of
round. Fasten off yarn.

MOTIF 4

New skills/Stitching motifs into position

These motifs are great for jazzing up any type of garment or accessory. The method for stitching the
motifs onto your item is the same whether it's a hand-knitted or store-bought item, though the
needle and thread you use may vary.

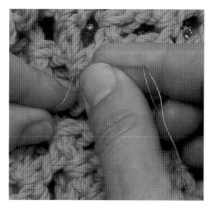

1 Pin finished motif into required position.

2 Thread sewing needle with thread that
tones in with motif, anchor thread at
back of garment.

3 Work in backstitch at outer edge of motif
until you have worked around the
outside of the shape.

Home Accessories

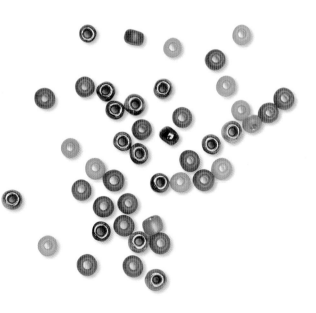

Project 25: Appliqué cushion

Almost too pretty to sit on, this generous cushion is worked in an aran-weight tweedy, natural yarn. The appliqué motifs, worked in a variety of sizes, are simple crochet discs in stripes and solids with contrasting beads to really add texture.

PILLOW PANEL
Make 2.

Using yarn A and larger hook, ch 48.
Row 1: Dc into third ch from hook and in each ch to end (46 dc). Ch 2, turn.
Rows 2–23: Dc into each st across. Ch 2, turn.
Row 24: Dc into each st across. Finish off. Make a second panel identical to the first.

before you start

MATERIALS
Yarn A: 2 x 100 g (3.5 oz) balls worsted-weight 100% wool (approximately 100 yds/100 m per ball) in ecru
Yarn B: 1 x 25 g (0.8 oz) ball worsted-weight 100% wool (approximately 100 yds/ 100 m per ball) in green
Yarn C: 1 x 25 g (0.8 oz) ball laceweight kid-mohair-and-silk blend (approximately 200 yds/210 m per ball) in lilac
Yarn D: 1 x 25 g (0.8 oz) ball worsted weight 100% wool (approximately 100 yds/ 100 m per ball) in ginger
Yarn E: 1 x 25 g (0.8 oz) ball laceweight kid-mohair-and-silk blend (approximately 200 yds/210 m per ball) in duck-egg blue
Yarn F: 1 x 25 g (0.8 oz) ball worsted weight 100% wool (approximately 100 yds/ 100 m per ball) in purple

Yarn G: 1 x 25 g (0.8 oz) ball laceweight kid-mohair-and-silk blend (approximately 200 yds/210 m per ball) in red
Approximately 60 purple beads
Approximately 100 red beads
16 in. (40-cm) square pillow form

HOOK SIZES
Main cushion—U.S. H-8 (5.0 mm);
Appliqué motifs—U.S. E-4 (3.5 mm)

GAUGE/TENSION
10 stitches and 6 rows to 4 in. (10 cm) in double-crochet pattern using larger hook

ABBREVIATIONS
bsc—beaded single crochet
ch—chain
dc—double crochet
rnd—round
sc—single crochet
sl st—slip stitch
st(s)—stitch(es)

Appliqué cushion motifs

MOTIF 1	MOTIF 2	MOTIF 3	MOTIF 4	MOTIF 5

Thread 15 red beads onto yarn B. With yarn B, ch 6. Sl st in farthest ch from hook to form a ring.

Thread 37 purple beads onto yarn B. With yarn B, ch 6. Sl st in farthest ch from hook to form a ring.

Thread 38 red beads onto yarn D. With yarn D, ch 6. Sl st in farthest ch from hook to form a ring.

Thread 15 purple beads onto yarn F. With yarn F, ch 6. Sl st in farthest ch from hook to form a ring.

(Shown with Motif 6 ov center.) Thread 24 red beads onto yarn E, and ch 6. Sl st in farthest c from hook to form a rir

 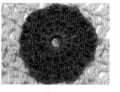 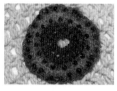 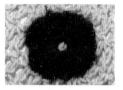 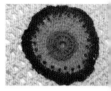

Rnd 1: Ch 1, work 15 sc into ring, join with sl st to first sc of rnd (15 sc).
Rnd 2: Ch 1, (sc, bsc) into each st around, join with sl st to first sc (30 sts).
Fasten off.

Rnd 1: Ch 1, work 15 sc into ring, join with sl st to first sc of rnd (15 sc).
Rnd 2: Ch 1, (sc, bsc) into each st around, join with sl st to first sc (30 sts). Change to yarn C.
Rnd 3: Ch 1, sc into each st around, join with sl st into first sc of rnd.
Rnd 4: Ch 1, sc, *2 sc into the next st, sc in the next st, repeat from * around, ending with sl st into first sc of rnd (45 sts). Change to yarn B.
Rnd 5: Ch 1, sc, *bsc in the next st, sc in the next st, repeat from * around, ending with sl st into first sc of rnd.
Fasten off.

Rnd 1: Ch 1, work 15 sc into ring, join with sl st to first sc of rnd (15 sc).
Rnd 2: Ch 1, (sc, bsc) into each st around, join with sl st to first sc (30 sts). Change to yarn E.
Rnd 3: Ch 1, sc in the first st, *bsc in the next st, sc in the next st, repeat from * around ending sl st into first sc of rnd.
Rnd 4: Ch 1, sc in the first st, *work 2 sc into next st, sc in the next st, repeat from * around, ending with sl st into first sc of rnd (45 sts). Change to yarn B.
Rnd 5: Ch 1, sc in the first st, *bsc in the next st, sc in the next st, repeat from * around, ending with sl st into first sc of rnd.
Fasten off.

Rnd 1: Ch 1, work 15 sc into ring, join with sl st to first sc of rnd (15 sts). Change to yarn G.
Rnd 2: Ch 1, work 2 sc into each st around, ending with sl st into first sc of rnd (30 sts). Change to yarn F.
Rnd 3: Ch 1, sc into each st around, ending with sl st into first st of rnd.
Rnd 4: Ch 1, *sc into next st, bsc in next st, repeat from * around, ending with sl st into first sc of rnd.
Fasten off.

Rnd 1: Ch 1, work 24 sc into ring, join with sl st into first sc of rnd (24 sts).
Rnd 2: Ch 1, work 2 sc into each st around, ending with sl st into first sc of rnd (48 sts).
Rnd 3: Ch 1, sc into eac st around, ending with st into first st of rnd.
Rnd 4: Ch 1, sc in the first st, *work 2 sc into next st, sc in the next s repeat from * around, ending with sl st into first sc of rnd (72 sts).
Rnd 5: Repeat rnd 3.
Rnd 6: Ch 1, 2 sc in the next st, *bsc in the nex st, sc in the next st, 2 s in the next st, repeat from * around, ending with sl st into first sc o rnd (96 sts, 24 beads). Change to yarn F.
Rnd 7: Repeat rnd 3.
Rnd 8: Ch 1, 3 sc in the next st, *2 sc in the ne st, 3 sc in the next st, repeat from * around, ending with sl st into first sc of rnd (120 sts). Fasten off.

MOTIF 6

(Shown over center of Motif 5.) With yarn B, ch 6. Sl st in farthest ch from hook to form a ring.

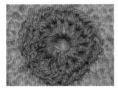

Rnd 1: Ch 1, work 15 sc into ring, join with sl st into first sc of rnd (15 sts).
Rnd 2: Ch 1, work 2 sc into each st around, ending with sl st into first sc of rnd (30 sts). Fasten off.

MOTIF 7

With yarn F, ch 6. Sl st in farthest ch from hook to form a ring.

Rnd 1: Ch 1, work 15 sc into ring, join with sl st into first sc of rnd (15 sts).
Rnd 2: Ch 1, work 2 sc into each st around, ending with sl st into first sc of rnd (30 sts).
Rnd 3: Ch 1, sc into each st around, ending with sl st into first sc of rnd. Fasten off.

FINISHING

Weave in all ends and tack motifs onto front panel of pillow. With wrong sides facing, sew panels together along 3 sides. Turn right side out, insert pillow form, and sew along last side.

Project 26: Beaded throw

Made up of contrasting colors and textured squares to form a checkered look, the soft and light kid-mohair-and-silk yarn works well with the textured tweedy 4-ply pure new wool. The red beads on the squares seem to blend the two colors together. Each square is worked separately so the throw can be easily made bigger.

before you start

MATERIALS

Yarn A: 5 x 25 g (0.8 oz) balls sport-weight wool (approximately 120 yds/110m per ball) in gray
Yarn B: 3 x 25 g (0.8 oz) balls laceweight kid-mohair-and-silk blend (approximately 230 yds/210 m
per ball) in red
Approximately 700 red beads

HOOK SIZE

U.S. E-4 (3.5mm)

GAUGE/TENSION

4 in. (10 cm) per square motif

FINISHED SIZE

28 in. (72 cm) by 36 in. (90 cm)

ABBREVIATIONS

bdc—beaded double crochet
bdc2tog—beaded double crochet 2 together
bdc3tog—beaded double crochet 3 together
ch—chain
lp(s)—loop(s)
rep—repeat
rnd—round
sc—single crochet
sl st—slip stitch
ws—wrong side

MOTIF

Thread beads onto yarn A. Make 32 beaded squares in yarn A and 31 unbeaded squares in yarn B.
Ch 6, join to form ring.

Rnd 1: Ch 1, (sc into ring, ch 15) 12 times, sl st to first sc.
Rnd 2: Sl st along in first 4 ch of ch 15 lp, ch 3, bdc2tog into same lp as follows: bring bead up to hook, (yo, insert hook in lp, yo, pull up a lp, yo pull through two lps) twice, yo, pull through all lps on hook. Bdc2tog made. *Ch 4, bdc3tog into same lp as follows: bring bead up to hook, (yo, insert hook in lp, yo, pull up a lp, yo pull through two lps) three times, yo, pull through all lps on hook. Bdc3tog made. (Ch 4, sc into next lp) twice, ch 4, bdc3tog into next lp, rep from * 3 more times, omitting bdc3tog at end of last rep, sl st into first bdc group.

Rnd 3: Sl st into corner lp, ch 3, bdc2tog into same lp, * ch 4, bdc3tog into same lp, (ch 4, sc into next ch lp, ch 4, bdc3tog into next lp) twice, rep from * 3 times more, omitting bdc3tog at end of last rep, sl st into first bdc group of rnd.
Fasten off.

JOINING

Using one motif of each color, hold motifs with ws together and yarn A motif facing you. Join yarn A with sl st in upper right corner lp of yarn A motif. Sc in same lp, ch 1. Sc in corresponding corner lp of yarn B motif behind. *Ch 1, sc in next ch lp of yarn A motif, ch 1, sc in next ch lp of yarn B motif. Rep from * until upper left corner of yarn B motif has been worked.
Fasten off.

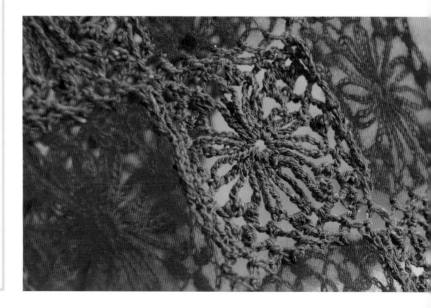

Project 27: Circular motif cushion

This project is chunky, funky, and fun! Worked using a super-size pure new wool, you will have made the front and back in no time. The fun feel to this cushion is also echoed with the addition of brightly colored wooden beads.

before you start

MATERIALS
3 x 100 g (3.5 oz) balls bulky
weight 100% wool (approximately
87 yds/80 m per ball) in ecru
Approximately 200 4-mm red
wooden beads
Approximately 50 10-mm multicolored wooden beads
One 20 in. (50 cm) diameter round
pillow form

HOOK SIZE
U.S. M/N-13 (9.0 mm)

GAUGE/TENSION
7 sts and 3 rows to 4 in. (10 cm)

FINISHED SIZE
20 in. (50 cm) diameter

ABBREVIATIONS
beg—beginning
ch—chain
dc—double crochet
rnd—round
sc—single crochet
sl st—slip stitch
st(s)—stitch(es)

PILLOW PANEL
Make 2.

Ch 6, sl st in farthest ch from hook to form a ring.
Rnd 1: Ch 2, work 12 dc into ring, sl st into ch 2 at beg of rnd (12 dc).
Rnd 2: Ch 2, work 2 dc into each dc of previous rnd, sl st into ch 2 at beg of rnd (24 dc).
Rnd 3: Ch 2, *2 dc into next st, dc into the next st, repeat from * around, sl st into beg ch 2 (36 dc).
Rnd 4: Ch 2, *2 dc into next st, dc into next 2 sts, repeat from * sl st into beg ch 2 (48 dc).
Rnd 5: Ch 2, *2 dc into next st, dc into next 3 sts, repeat from * sl st into beg ch 2 (60 dc).
Rnd 6: Ch 2, *2 dc into next st, dc into next 4 sts, repeat from * sl st into beg ch 2 (72 dc).
Rnd 7: Ch 2, *2 dc into next st, dc into next 5 sts, repeat from * sl st into beg ch 2 (84 dc). Finish off.

FRONT PANEL BEADING
Stitch 1 red bead to top of each dc on rnd 2.
Stitch 1 multicolored bead to top of every third dc on rnd 3.
Stitch 1 red bead to top of each dc on rnd 4.
Stitch 1 multicolored bead to top of every fourth dc on rnd 5
Stitch 1 red bead to top of every dc on rnd 6.

ASSEMBLY
Place front and back panels so that wrong sides are facing. In any st of rnd 7, insert hook in a st from both the front and back panel at the same time, and join with a sl st. Ch 1, sc in the same st and in each st around, making sure to catch both the front and back panels in each st.

Once you have worked approximately halfway around the edge, insert the pillow form and complete the rnd as before, ending with a sl st in the first sc of rnd. Finish off and weave in ends.

Project 28: Beaded mat

These place settings are fun and easy to make. Crocheted in worsted-weight cotton yarn, they can be easily popped in the washing machine. Change the colors to coordinate them with your favorite crockery or dining area décor.

before you start

MATERIALS
50 g (1.75 oz) worsted-weight cotton (approximately 64 yds/58 m per ball) in cream
Approximately 350 silver-lined glass beads

HOOK SIZE
U.S. H-8 (5.0 mm)

GAUGE/TENSION
3.25 in. (8.5 cm) across one stitch repeat, 11 rows per 3 in. (7.5 cm).

FINISHED SIZE
12 x 8 in. (30 x 20 cm)

ABBREVIATIONS
bsc—beaded single crochet
ch—chain
dc—double crochet
lp—loop
rep—repeat
rnd—round
sc—single crochet
sk—skip
sl st—slip stitch
st(s)—stitch(es)

PATTERN
Row 1: Ch 46, sc in second ch from hook and in each ch to end, turn (45 sc).
Row 2: Ch 1, sc in first 3 sts, *ch 5, (sk 2, dc in next st) 3 times, ch 5, sk 2, sc in next 3 sts. Rep from * across, turn.
Row 3: Ch 1, sc in first 3 sts, *ch 5, sc in ch lp, sc in next 3 dc, sc in ch loop, ch 5, sc in next 3 sc. Rep from * across, turn.
Row 4: Ch 1, sc in first 3 sts, *ch 5, sk first sc, sc in next 3 sc, sk next sc, ch 5, sc in next 3 sc. Rep from * across, turn.
Row 5: Ch 1, sc in first 3 sts, *(ch 2, dc in next sc) 3 times ch 2, sc in next 3 sc. Rep from * across, turn.
Row 6: Ch 1, sc across, working a sc in each sc, 2 sc in each ch lp, and sc in each dc. Turn (45 sc).
Rows 7–21: Rep rows 2 through 6 three more times, then break off yarn.

BORDER
String all beads onto yarn.
Rnd 1: With wrong side facing, join with sl st in any st. Ch 1, sc in each st and end of each row around, working 3 sc in the corners. Do not turn.
Rnd 2: Ch 1, bsc in each st around, working 3 bsc in each corner.
Rnd 3: Ch 1, sc in each st around, working 3 sc in each corner.
Rnd 4: Rep rnd 2.

Finish off and weave in ends.

Project 29: Floor cushion

This textured floor cushion is worked in a beautiful pure new wool, aran-weight tweedy yarn. The checkerboard pattern is created by working evenly around the front or back of the stitches. The center panels have been framed with a simple beaded border worked in separate sections.

before you start

MATERIALS

6 x 50 g (1.75 oz) balls worsted-weight 100% wool (approximately 123 yds/113m per ball) in green

800 clear glass beads

24 in. (60 cm) square pillow form

HOOK SIZE

U.S. H-8 (5.0 mm)

GAUGE/TENSION

13 stitches and 8 rows to 4 in. (10 cm) over textured pattern

FINISHED SIZE

23 in. (58 cm) square

ABBREVIATIONS

bpdc—back post double crochet

bsc—beaded single crochet

ch—chain

dc—double crochet

fpdc—front post double crochet

rep—repeat

rnd—round

rs—right side

sc—single crochet

sl st—slip stitch

st(s)—stitch(es)

ws—wrong side

yo—yarn over

TEXTURED PATTERN (FRONT PANEL)

Ch 64.

Row 1 (ws): Dc into third ch from the hook and in each ch to end. Turn.

Row 2 (rs): Ch 2, miss first st * 4 fpdc, 4 bpdc, rep from * 6 more times. 4 fpdc, dc into top of turning ch.

Row 3: Ch 2, miss first st * 4 bpdc, 4 fpdc, rep from * 6 times. 4 bpdc, ending with dc into top of turning ch.

Row 4: Rep row 2.

Row 5: Rep row 2.

Row 6: Rep row 3.

Row 7: Rep row 2.

Rows 8–37: Rep rows 2 through 7 another 5 times.

BEADED BORDER

Thread beads onto yarn.

With ws of work facing, join with sl st to lower right hand corner and work up the right hand side.

Rnd 1 (rs): Ch 1, work 2 bsc around post of dc at end of row 1, * bsc around post of next dc at end of next row, 2 bsc around post of dc at end of next row, rep from * up side of piece. Work 3 bsc in corner, bsc in each dc across top, 3 bsc in corner, 2 bsc around post of dc in row 37, rep from * to * down third side. Work 3 bsc in corner, bsc in unworked lps of beginning ch, 3 bsc in last corner. Join with sl st to first bsc of rnd.

Rnd 2 (ws): Ch 1, sc into each bsc of previous round, working 3 sc into each corner, join with sl st to first sc of rnd.

Rnd 3: Ch 1, bsc into each sc of previous round, working 3 bsc into each corner, join with sl st into first bsc of rnd.

Rnd 4: Rep rnd 2.

Rnd 5: Rep rnd 3.

Fasten off and weave in ends.

BACK PANEL

Ch 61.

Row 1: Dc into third ch from hook and in each ch to end (60 sts includes turning ch.

Row 2: Ch 2, turn. Dc into each st across.

Rows 3–28: Rep row 2.

SINGLE CROCHET BORDER

With ws of work facing, join with sl st to lower right hand corner and work up the right hand side.

Rnd 1: Ch 1, work 2 sc around post of dc at end of row 1, *sc around post of dc at end of next row, 2 sc around post of dc at end of next row, rep from * up side of piece. Work 3 sc in corner, sc in each dc across top, 3 sc in corner, 2 sc around post of dc at end of row 37, rep from * to * down third side. Work 3 sc in corner, sc in unworked lps of beginning ch, 3 sc in last corner. Join with sl st to first sc of rnd.

Rnd 2: Ch 1, sc into each sc of previous rnd, working 3sc into each corner, join with sl st to first sc of rnd.

Rnds 3–5: Rep rnd 2.

Fasten off yarn and weave in ends.

FINISHING

With ws of panels held together, sew along 3 sides. Insert pillow form, and sew up last side.

New skills/Front and back stem double crochet stitch

This is a technique used to add texture and pattern to your crochet fabric by simply working crochet stitches around either the front or back of the stem of the stitch in the row below.

Front post double crochet

1 Yarn over as normal, insert hook from the front right to left around the back of the stem of the stitch instead of into the top, yarn over and draw round stem, back to start position.

2 Yarn over and complete double as normal.

Back post double

1 Yarn over as normal, insert hook from the back right to left around the front of the stem of the stitch instead of into the top, yarn over and draw round stem, back to start position.

2 Yarn over and complete double as normal.

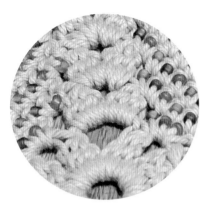

Project 30: Coasters

This project is quick and easy to make, and the beaded DK cotton gives a nice weight to the coasters. It's also a fun way to use up all your odd bits of wool, using different types of yarn to truly make them your own.

before you start

MATERIALS

For 2 coasters, one 50 g (1.75 oz) ball DK-weight 100% cotton (approximately 97 yds/89 m per ball) in ecru

Approximately 70 beads for edge-only coaster

Approximately 150 beads for panel coaster

HOOK SIZE

U.S. G-6 (4.0 mm)

GAUGE/TENSION

Round 1 measures 2 in. (5 cm) across between ch 2 loops

FINISHED SIZE

Approximately 5 in. (12.5 cm) square

ABBREVIATIONS

beg cl—beginning cluster

bsc—beaded single crochet

ch—chain

cl—cluster

dc—double crochet

sc—single crochet

sl st—slip stitch

sp—space

yo—yarn over

BEADED EDGE COASTER

Thread 70 beads onto yarn. Ch 8, join with sl st in farthest ch from hook to make a ring.

Rnd 1: Make beg cl into ring as follows: ch 3, *yo, insert hook, yo, pull up a loop, yo pull through 2 loops on hook, repeat from * once, yo, pull through all 3 loops on hook. Beg cl made. Ch 5.
Make cl as follows: repeat from * to * 3 times, yo, pull through all 4 loops on hook. Cl made. Ch 2, (cl, ch 5, cl, ch 2) three more times. Join with sl st in 3rd ch of beg cl.

Rnd 2: Sl st into first ch 5 sp, (beg cl, ch 2, cl) in same sp, ch 2, 3 sc into the next ch 2 sp, ch 2, *(cl, ch 2, cl) into ch 5 sp, ch 2, 3 sc into next ch 2 sp, ch 2, rep from * around. Join with sl st to 3rd ch of beg cl.

Rnd 3: Sl st into first ch 2 sp, (beg cl, ch 2, cl) in same sp, *ch 2, 2 sc into ch 2 sp, sc into each of the next 3 sc, 2 sc into next ch 2 sp, ch 2, (cl, ch 2, cl) in ch 2 sp, rep from * around. Join with sl st into 3rd ch of beg cl.

Rnd 4: Sl st into first ch 2 sp, (beg cl, ch 2, cl) in same sp, *ch 2, 2 sc into ch 2 sp, sc into each of the next 7 sc, 2 sc into next ch 2 sp, ch 2, (cl, ch 2, cl) in ch 2 sp, rep from * around. Join with sl st into 3rd ch of beg cl.

Rnd 5: Sl st into first ch 2 sp, (beg cl, ch 2, cl) in same sp, *ch 2, 2 bsc into ch 2 sp, bsc into each of the next 11 sc, 2 bsc into next ch 2 sp, ch 2, (cl, ch 2, cl) in ch 2 sp, rep from * around. Join with sl st into 3rd ch of beg cl. Fasten off yarn.

BEADED PANEL COASTER

Thread 150 beads onto yarn. Ch 8, join with sl st in farthest ch from hook to make a ring.

Rnd 1: Make beg cl into ring: ch 3, *yo, insert hook, yo, pull up a loop, yo pull through 2 loops on hook, repeat from * once, yo, pull through all 3 loops on hook. Beg cl made. Ch 5.
Make cl: repeat from * to * 3 times, yo, pull through all 4 loops on hook. Cl made. Ch 2, (cl, ch 5, cl, ch 2) three more times. Join with sl st in 3rd ch of beg cl.

Rnd 2: Sl st into first ch 5 sp, (beg cl, ch 2, cl) in same sp, ch 2, 3 bsc into the next ch 2 sp, ch 2, *(cl, ch 2, cl) into ch 5 sp, ch 2, 3 sc into next ch 2 sp, ch 2, rep from * around. Join with sl st to 3rd ch of beg cl.

Rnd 3: Sl st into first ch 2 sp, (beg cl, ch 2, cl) in same sp, *ch 2, 2 bsc into ch 2 sp, bsc into each of the next 3 sc, 2 bsc into next ch 2 sp, ch 2, (cl, ch 2, cl) in ch 2 sp, rep from * around. Join with sl st into 3rd ch of beg cl.

Rnd 4: Sl st into first ch 2 sp, (beg cl, ch 2, cl) in same sp, *ch 2, 2 bsc into ch 2 sp, bsc into each of the next 7 sc, 2 bsc into next ch 2 sp, ch 2, (cl, ch 2, cl) in ch 2 sp, rep from * around. Join with sl st into 3rd ch of beg cl.

Rnd 5: Sl st into first ch 2 sp, (beg cl, ch 2, cl) in same sp, *ch 2, 2 bsc into ch 2 sp, bsc into each of the next 11 sc, 2 bsc into next ch 2 sp, ch 2, (cl, ch 2, cl) in ch 2 sp, rep from * around. Join with sl st into 3rd ch of beg cl. Fasten off yarn.

Trims

If you want to liven up a plain or shop-bought item—whether a garment, wearable accessory or home accessory, try making or adapting these trims. In no time at all, you'll have the length you need, and then you can simply attach by sewing or crocheting it on for instant results that look great! Change the yarn and bead colors to complement your item.

Beaded trim 1

MATERIALS

Yarn A: sport-weight 100% wool (approximately 120 yds/110 m per ball in dark purple
Yarn B: 25 g laceweight kid-mohair-and-silk blend (approximately 230 yds/ 210 m per ball)in violet
two 10-mm glass beads per in. (2.5 cm) of trim length

FINISHED SIZE

2 repeats per in. (2.5 cm), 1 inch (2.5 cm) wide

ABBREVIATIONS

bch—beaded chain
ch—chain
lp—loop
sc—single crochet
sk—skip

PATTERN

Row 1: Using yarn A, ch a multiple of 3 sts. Sc in 6th ch from hook. (Ch 2, sk 2, sc in next ch) across. Fasten off.

Row 2: Using double strand of yarn B as one, thread beads onto yarn. * Work (2 sc, ch, bch, ch, 2 sc in same lp) across. Fasten off.

Beaded trim 2

PATTERN

Using yarn A, ch a multiple of 3 sts plus 1.

Row 1: Sc in 2nd ch from hook and each ch to end, turn.

Row 2: Ch 1, sc in back lp of each st across, turn.

Row 3: Ch 1, sc in front lp of each st across. Fasten off.

Thread beads onto yarn B.

Row 4: Using yarn B, sc in first 2 sts, bsc in next st, (ch 10, sk 5 sts, bch in next st across. Fasten off.

Row 5: Using yarn C, sc in 1st sc of row 4. (Ch 10, sk 5 sts of row 3, sc in next st) across.

MATERIALS

Yarn A: sport-weight 100% wool (approximately 120 yds/110 m per ball in lavender
Yarn B: sport-weight 100% wool (approximately 120 yds/110 m per ball in pink
Yarn C: sport-weight 100% wool (approximately 120 yds/110 m per ball in red
10-mm beads, 1 per in. (2.5 cm) of trim length

FINISHED SIZE

1 repeat per in. (2.5 cm)
1.5 in. (3.75 cm) wide

ABBREVIATIONS

ch—chain
bsc—beaded single crochet
sc—single crochet
sk—skip
lp—loop
st(s)—stitch(es)

Beaded trim 3

MATERIALS

25 g ball sport-weight 100% wool (approximately 120 yds/110 m per ball in pink

Small white beads, 10 per in. of trim length

FINISHED SIZE

3 repeat per 8 inches (20 cm), 1.75 inch (4.5 cm) wide

ABBREVIATIONS

bsc—beaded single crochet
ch—chain
dec—decrease
lp—loop
rs—right side
sc—single crochet
ws—wrong side

PATTERN

Row 1 (rs): Ch 5, sc in 2nd ch from hook and each across, turn (4 sc).

Row 2 (ws): Ch 1, decrease (dec) as follows: (insert hook in next st and pull up a loop) twice, yo, pull through all 3 lps on hook. Dec made. Sc in next st, 2 sc in last st, turn (4 sts).

Row 3: Ch 1, 2 sc in first st, sc in next, dec across next 2 sts, turn (4 sts).

Row 4: Repeat row 2.

Row 5: Repeat row 3.

Row 6: Repeat row 2

Row 7: Ch 1, sc in each st across, turn (4 sts).

Row 8: Repeat row 3.

Row 9: Repeat row 2.

Row 10: Repeat row 3.

Row 11: Repeat row 2.

Row 12: Repeat row 3.

Row 13: Repeat rrow 7.

Repeat rows 2–13 until trim is desired length.

CIRCLES

Make one per inch of finished trim length.

Using either yarn A or B, ch 4, join with sl st in ch farthest from hook to form ring.

Rnd 1: Ch 1, work 8 sc in ring, join with sl st to first sc of round.

Rnd 2: Ch 1, 2 sc in each st around, join with sl st to first sc of round. Finish off.

TRIM

Thread beads onto yarn C.

Row 1: Using yarn C, (ch 7, sc in any edge st of a circle) to desired length, ending ch 8, turn.

Rows 2–4: Sk first ch, (7 sc, bsc) across, ending with 7 sc, turn. Fasten off at end of row 4.

Beaded trim 4

MATERIALS

Yarn A: sport-weight 100% wool (approximately 120 yds/110 m per ball in rose

Yarn B: sport-weight 100% wool (approximately 120 yds/110 m per ball in red

Yarn C: sport-weight 100% wool (approximately 120 yds/110 m per ball in pink

Small red beads, 3 per inch (2.5 cm) of trim length

FINISHED SIZE

1 repeat per in. (2.5 cm), 1.5 in. (4.5 cm) wide

ABBREVIATIONS

ch—chain
bch—beaded chai
sc—single crochet
sk—skip

Yarn directory

Below is a list of the specific yarns and beads used to make the projects. However, if you cannot find any of these yarns or simply wish to make a project in a different yarn, use the information supplied at the beginning of each project, where you will find the quantity, weight, and fiber content of the yarns. Additional advice on substituting yarns can be found on pages 12–13.

WEARABLE ACCESSORIES

Project 1: Beaded ruffle scarf
Yarns: Rowan kid classic: 847 (cherry red); Rowan kidsilk haze 595 (liqueur).
Beads: 100 multicolored large glass beads.

Project 2: Lace-effect shawl
Yarns: Rowan DK felted tweed 146 (herb); Rowan kidsilk haze 585 (nightly); Rowan kidsilk haze 582 (trance); Rowan kidsilk haze 597 (jelly); Rowan kidsilk haze 592 (heavenly).
Beads: Rowan j3001008.

Project 3: Wrist warmers
Yarn: Rowan kidsilk haze 582 (trance).
Beads: Rowan j3001006.

Project 4: Pashmina
Yarns: Rowan kid classic 840 (crystal); Rowan kidsilk haze 589 (majestic); Rowan kidsilk haze 592 (heavenly).
Beads: Rowan j3001014.

Project 5: Beaded string bag
Yarn: Rowan handknit DK cotton 318 (seafarer).
Beads: Nottingham bead company: purple 8-mm wooden beads; pink 6-mm wooden beads; natural 10-mm wooden beads.

Project 6: Shoulder bag
Yarns: Rowan big wool 007 (smoky); Rowan big wool 008 (black); Rowan kidsilk haze 600 (dewberry).
Beads: Approx. 120 pewter glass beads.

Project 7: Evening bag
Yarn: Rowan cotton glace 816 (mocha choc).
Beads: Beadworks: 240 dark turquoise glass beads; 280 green glass beads; 220 silvery green glass beads.

Project 8: Flower pin corsage
Yarns: Rowan Yorkshire tweed 4-ply 286 (graze); Rowan Yorkshire tweed 4-ply 268 (enchant); Rowan kidsilk haze 605 (smoke).
Beads: Rowan j3001017.

Project 9: Beaded beanie
Yarn: Rowan DK wool cotton 900 (antique).
Beads: Rowan j3001022.

Project 10: Twenties-inspired scarf
Yarn: Rowan kidsilk haze 581 (meadow)
Beads: Approx. 280 matt green glass beads (Rowan j3001022).

Project 11: Beaded beret
Yarn: Rowan 4-ply soft 370 (whisper).
Beads: Approx 260 pewter glass beads (Rowan j3001006).

Project 12: Textured beaded bag
Yarns: Rowan summer tweed 526 (angel); Rowan summer tweed 528 (brilliant).
Beads: Nottingham beads company: 144 pink 8-mm wooden beads.

Project 13: Beaded necklace
Yarn: Rowan lurex shimmer 333 (pewter).
Beads: Rowan j3001006.

Project 14: Earflap hat
Yarns: Rowan Yorkshire tweed chunky 557 (olive oil); Rowan kidsilk haze 582 (trance); Rowan kidsilk haze 584 (villain); Rowan kidsilk haze 592 (heavenly); Rowan kidsilk haze 581 (meadow); Rowan kidsilk haze 588 (drab).
Beads: 50 multicolored, mixed-size glass beads.

Project 15: Beaded head band
Yarn: Rowan handknit DK cotton 251 (ecru).
Beads: Rowan j3001017.

Project 16: Brooch and pendant
Yarn: Rowan Yorkshire tweed 4-ply 264 (barley).
Beads: 9 medium glass beads—various colors; Beadworks: 9 orange small beads.

GARMENTS

Project 17: Box crew-neck
Yarn: Rowan wool cotton 952 (hiss); Rowan 4-ply soft 387 (rain cloud).
Beads: Rowan j3001006.

Project 18: Slash-neck vest
Yarn: Rowan summer tweed 537 (summer berry).
Beads: Nottingham bead company: 60 purple 6-mm beads.

Project 19: Halter-neck top
Yarn: Rowan cotton glace 811 (tickle).
Beads: Approx. 70 purple (Rowan j3001014); approx. 70 blue (Rowan j3001013).

Project 20: Cobweb shrug
Yarn: Rowan kidsilk haze 582 (trance).
Beads: Rowan j3001006.

Project 21: Beaded tunic
Yarns: Rowan cotton rope 062 (fruit gum); Rowan handknit DK cotton 303 (sugar)
Beads: Approx. 400 white beads (Rowan j3001016).

Project 22: Bikini top
Yarn: Rowan denim 225 (Nashville)
Beads: Approx. 250 turquoise glass beads (Rowan j3001013).

Project 23: Cap-sleeved wrap
Yarn: Rowan cotton glace 730 (Oyster)
Beads: 248 pewter beads (Rowan j3001006); Beadworks: 248 orange beads.

Project 24: Motifs for sweaters
Yarns: Rowan Yorkshire tweed 4-ply 273 (glory); Rowan Yorkshire tweed 4-ply 286 (graze); C: Rowan Yorkshire tweed 4-ply 271 (cheerful); Rowan Yorkshire tweed 4-ply 263 (dessicated); Rowan kidsilk haze 600 (dewberry); Rowan kidsilk haze 582 (trance); Rowan kidsilk haze 606 (candy girl); Rowan kidsilk haze 597 (jelly); Rowan lurex shimmer 336 (gleam); Rowan lurex shimmer 333 (pewter); Rowan lurex shimmer 335 (bronze).

HOME ACCESSORIES

Project 25: Appliqué cushion
Yarn: Rowan Yorkshire tweed aran 417 (tusk); Rowan Yorkshire tweed 4-ply 273 (glory); Rowan Yorkshire tweed 4-ply 286 (graze); Rowan kidsilk haze 606 (candy girl); Rowan kidsilk haze 582 (trance); Rowan kidsilk haze 600 (dewberry).
Beads: Approx. 80 purple (Rowan j3001019); Approx. 60 red (Rowan j3001018).

Project 26: Beaded throw
Yarns: Rowan Yorkshire tweed 4-ply 268 (enchant); Rowan kidsilk haze 606 (candy girl).
Beads: Rowan j3001018.

Project 27: Circular cushion
Yarn: Rowan big wool 001 (hot white).
Beads: Nottingham beads company: 152 red wooden 4-mm beads.

Project 28: Beaded mat
Yarn: Rowan handknit DK cotton 251 (ecru).
Beads: Beadworks: clear, small glass beads

Project 29: Floor cushion
Yarn: Rowan Yorkshire tweed DK 347 (skip).
Beads: Rowan j3001008

Project 30: Coasters
Yarn: Rowan handknit DK cotton 205 (ecru)
Beads: Rowan j3001022; Rowan j3001019; Beadworks: small orange glass beads.

Trims
Yarns: Rowan cotton glace 816 (mocha choc); Rowan kidsilk haze 600 (dewberry); Rowan cotton glace 811 (tickle); Rowan handknit cotton 215 (rosso); Rowan handknit cotton 303 (slick); Rowan lurex shimmer 336 (gleam); Rowan kidsilk haze 606 (hot pink); Rowan kidsilk haze 596 (marmalade); Rowan kidsilk haze 583 (blushes); Rowan kidsilk haze (shell); Rowan cotton glace 747 (candy girl).
Beads: John Lewis Partnership: mix of multi-shaped glass beads; Rowan 3001018; Rowan j300101016.

Resources

Alabama

Heidi's Yarnhaus
Mobile, AL 36609
251-342-0088
www.yarnhaus.com

Memory Hagler Knitting
Birmingham, AL 35216
205-822-7875

Yarn Expressions
Huntsville, AL 35802-2274
256-881-0260

Alaska

Changing Threads
326 Third Ave
Skagway, AK 99840
907-983-3700
www.changingthreads.com

Knitting Frenzy
Anchorage, AK 99503
907-563-2717

A Weaver's Yarn
Fairbanks, AK 99708
907-322-5050

Arizona

A Back Door Bead and Yarn Co.
Tucson, AZ 85741
520-742-0377
www.bdbeads.com

Knitting in Scottsdale
Scottsdale, AZ 85254
480-951-9942

Unravel Yarns
Flagstaff, AZ 86001
928-556-9276
www.unravelshop.com

Arkansas

Designing Yarns
Jonesboro, AR 72401
870-972-9537

Hand Held Knitting Gallery
Fayetteville, AR 72701
479-582-2910

Yarn Mart
Little Rock, AR 72207
501-666-6505

California

Ancient Pathways
Fresno, CA 93728
559-264-1874

Black Sheep Knitting
Los Angeles, CA 90028
323-464-2253

The Grove at Juniper and 30th
San Diego, CA 92104
619-284-7684

Knitting Room
San Jose, CA 95124
408-264-7229

Knitting Basket
Oakland, CA 94611
510-339-6295
www.theknittingbasket.com

The Knitty Gritty
Anaheim, CA 92805
714-778-2340
www.theknittygritty.com

Paper Habit
Modesto, CA 95350
209-567-0605

Stash
Berkeley, CA 94707
510-558-9276
contact@stashyarn.com

Straw Into Gold
160 23rd Street
Richmond, CA 94804

The Swift Stitch
Santa Cruz, CA 95060
831-427-9276

Trendsetter Yarns
16745 Saticoy Street, Suite 101
Van Nuys, CA 91406
818-780-5497
www.trendsetteryarns.com

Unicorn Books and Crafts, Inc.
1338 Ross Street
Petaluma, CA 94954
800-BUY-YARN
www.unicornbooks.com

Urban Knitting Studio
San Francisco, CA 94102
415-552-5333
www.urbanknitting.com

Wildfiber
Santa Monica, CA 90404
310-458-2748

The Yarn Boutique
Lafayette, CA 94549
925-283-7377
www.yarnboutique.us

Colorado

A Knitted Peace
Littleton, CO 80120
303-730-0366

Showers of Flowers
6900 West Colfax Avenue
Lakewood, CO 80215
www.showersofflowers.com

Strawberry Tree
Denver, CO 80222
303-759-4244

Connecticut

Mystic River Yarns
Mystic, CT 06355
860-536-4305

Yarns Down Under
Deep River, CT 06417
860-526-9986
www.yarnsdownunder.com

Yarns with a Twist
Chaplin, CT 06235
860-455-9986
yarnswithatwist@yahoo.com

Delaware

Knit2purl2
Newark, Delaware 19711
302-737-4917
www.knit2purl2.com

Florida

Elegant Stitches
Miami, FL 33176
305-232-4005

Knit 'n Knibble
Tampa, FL 33629
813-254-5648

Yarn Works
Gainesville, FL 32609
352-337-9965

Georgia

In Stitches
Augusta, GA 30907
706-868-9276

The Knitting Emporium
Kennesaw, GA 30144
770-421-1919

Needle Nook
Atlanta, GA 30329-3449
404-325-0068

Hawaii

Aloha Yarn
Kaneohe, HI 96744
808-234-5865

Big Island Bernina
Hilo, HI 96720
808-929-0034

Isle Knit
Honolulu, HI 96813
808-533-0853

Idaho

Drop a Stitch
Boise, ID 83702
208-331-3767

Isabell's Needlepoint
Ketchum, ID 83340
208-725-0408

Sheep to Shawl
Twin Falls, ID 83301
208-735-8425

Illinois

Arcadia Knitting
Chicago, IL 60640
773-293-1211

Sunflower Samplings
Crystal Lake, IL 60014
815-455-2919

Three Bags Full
Northbrook, IL 60062
847-291-9933

Indiana

Mass. Ave. Knit Shop
Indianapolis, IN 46203
317-638-1833

River Knits
Lafayette, IN 47901
765-742-5648

Sheep St. Fibers, Inc.
Morgantown, IN 46160
812-597-5648

Iowa
Creative Corner
W. Des Moines, IA 50265
515-255-7262

The Knitting Shop
Iowa City, IA 52240
319-337-4920

Three Oaks Knits
Cedar Falls, IA 50613
319-266-6221

Kansas
Laura May's Cottage
Lindsborg, KS 67456
785-227-3948

Wildflower Yarns and Knitwear
Manhattan, KS 66502
785-537-1826
www.wildflowerknits.com

Yarn Barn
Lawrence, KS 66044
785-842-4333

Kentucky
Carma Needlecraft, Inc.
Louisville, KY 40222
502-425-4170

The Stitche Niche, Inc.
Lexington, KY 40503
859-277-2604

Stone's Throw Artisans
Georgetown, KY 40324
502-867-5897

Louisiana
The Yarn Nook
Crowley, LA 70526
337-783-5565

Maine
Cityside Yarn Co.
Bangor, ME 04401
207-990-1455

Knitwit Yarn Shop and Cafe
Portland, ME 04101
207-774-6444

Water Street Yarns
Hallowell, ME 04347
207-622-5500

Maryland
Keep Me in Stitches!
Frederick, MD 21701
240-379-7740

Woolstock
Glyndon, MD 21071
410-517-1020

Woolworks
Baltimore, MD 21209
410-337-9030

Massachusetts
Sheep to Shore
Nantucket, MA 02554
508-228-0038

Wild and Woolly Studio
Lexington, MA 02420
781-861-7717
wwoolly@aol.com

Windsor Button
Boston, MA 02111
617-482-4969
www.windsorbutton.com

Michigan
City Knits
Detroit, MI 48202
313-872-9665

Knit a Round Yarn Shop
Ann Arbor, MI 48105
734-998-3771

The Wool & the Floss
Grosse Point, MI 48230
313-882-9110

Minnesota
Linden Hills Yarns
Minneapolis, MN 55410
612-929-1255

Three Kitten Yarn Shoppe
St Paul, MN 55118
651-457-4969

Yarnworks
Grand Rapids, MN 55744
218-327-1898

Mississippi
Knit Wits
Jackson, MS 39211
601-957-9098

Missouri
Chris' Needlecraft Supplies
Chesterfield, MO 63017
314-205-8766

Hearthstone Knits
St. Louis, MO 63123
314-849-9276

Simply Fibers Ltd.
Springfield, MO 65807
417-881-Yarn

Montana
Knit 'n Needle
Whitefish, MT 59937
406-862-6390

Pam's Knit 'n Stitch
Great Falls, MT 59401
406-761-4652

Stix
Bozeman, MT 59715
406-556-5786
www.stix.com

Nebraska
Personal Threads
Omaha, NE 68114
402-391-7733

Plum Nelly
Hastings, NE 68901
402-462-2490

String of Purls
Omaha, NE 68114
402-393-5648

Nevada
Deluxe Yarns etc.
Reno, NV 89509
775-322-1244

Gail Knits
Las Vegas, NV 89117
702-838-7713

Wooly Wonders
Las Vegas, NV 89121
702-547-1661

New Hampshire
Charlotte's Web
Exeter, NH 03833
603-778-1417

The Elegant Ewe
Concord, NH 03301
603-226-0066
www.elegantewe.com

Spinning Yarns
Dover, NH 03820
603-740-6476

Westminster Fibers
4 Townsend West, Unit 8
Nashua, NH 03063

New Jersey
The Knitting Room
Medford, NJ 08055
609-654-9003

The Knitting Store
Cherry Hill, NJ 08003
856-751-7750
theknittingstore@comcast.net

Wooly Monmouth
Red Bank, NJ 07701
732-224-YARN
www.woolymonmouth.com

New Mexico
Three Stitchers
Clovis, NM 88101
505-762-0295

Village Wools
Albuquerque, NM 87110
505-883-2919

The Yarn Shop
Taos, NM 87571
505-758-9341

New York
Downtown Yarns
New York, NY 10009
212-995-5991

Knit 'n Purl
Rochester, NY 14618
585-442-7420

Knitting Fever, Inc.
35 Debevoise Avenue
Roosevelt, NY 11575
www.knittingfever.com
Rock City Yarn
Woodstock, NY 12498
845-679-9600

North Carolina
Knit One Smock Too
Winston Salem, NC 27104
336-765-9099
The Sewing Bird
Charlotte, NC 28209
704-676-0076
This and That
Greensboro, NC 27408
336-275-0044

North Dakota
Bandanas and Bows
Medora, ND 58645
701-623-4347

Ohio
The Knitting Room
Cleveland, OH 44122
216-464-8450
Peach Mountain Studio
Cincinnati, OH 45243
513-271-3191
Wolfe Fiber Arts, Inc.
Columbus, OH 43212
614-487-9980

Oklahoma
Gourmet Yarn Co.
Oklahoma City, OK 73120
405-286-3737
Naturally Needlepoint
Tulsa, OK 74105
918-747-8838
Sealed with a Kiss, Inc.
Guthrie, OK 73044
405-282-8649

Oregon
Artistic Needles
Salem, OR 97301
503-589-1502
The Cozy Ewe
Oregon City, OR 97045
503-723-5255

Knit Shop, Inc.
Eugene, OR 97405
541-434-0430
Northwest Wools
Portland, OR 97219
503-244-5024

Pennsylvania
Knitter's Dream
Harrisburg, PA 17112
717-599-7665
www.knittersdream.com
Pittsburgh Knit and Bead
Pittsburgh, PA 15217
412-421-7522
Unique Kolours, LLC
28 N. Bacton Hill Road
Malvern, PA 19355
800-252-3934
www.uniquekolours.com
Yarn Basket
Chambersburg, PA 17201
717-263-3236

Rhode Island
Craft Corner
Woonsocket, RI 02895
401-762-3233
Yarn Outlet
Pawtucket, RI 02860
401-722-5600

South Carolina
Island Knits
The Island Shops
Pawleys Island, SC 29585
843-235-0110
Knit
Charleston, SC 29403
843-937-8500

South Dakota
Ben Franklin Crafts
Mitchell, SD 57301
605-996-5464

Tennessee
Angel Hair Yarn Co.
Nashville, TN 37215
615-269-8833
Genuine Purl
Chattanooga, TN 37405
423-267-7335

The Yarn Studio
Memphis, TN 38104
901-276-5442

Texas
Desert Designs Knitz
Dallas, TX 75254
972-392-9276
Hill Country Weavers
Austin, TX 78704
512-707-7396
Nimble Fingers
Houston, TX 77024
713-722-7244

Utah
Heindselman's
Provo, UT 84601
801-373-5193
Judy's Novelty Wool
Centerville, UT 84014
801-298-1356
Soul Spun
Salt Lake City, UT 84109
801-746-5094

Vermont
Naked Sheep
Bennington, VT 05201
802-440-9653
Pine Ledge Fiber Studio
Fairfax, VT 05454
802-849-9731
River Muse Yarn
Johnson, VT 05656
802-635-9851
rivermuse@msn.com

Virginia
Knitting Basket
Richmond, VA 23226
804-282-2909
www.theknittingbasket.biz
Knitting Sisters
Williamsburg, VA 23185
757-258-5005
www.knittingsisters.com
Knitwits
Virginia Beach, VA 23464
757-495-6600

Washington
Acorn Street Yarn Shop
Seattle, WA 98105
206-525-1726
Amanda's Art Yarns
Poulsbo, WA 98370
360-779-3666
Hank & Bolt Co.
Bellingham, WA 98225
360-733-7836
King Cole and Cascade Yarns
PO Box 58168
Tukwila, WA 98188
www.cascadeyarns.com
Lamb's Ear
Tacoma, WA 98408
253-472-7695
www.lambsearfarm.com

Washington, DC
Stitch DC, Inc.
Washington, DC 20003
202-487-4337

West Virginia
Kanawha City Yarn Co.
Charleston, WV 25304
304-926-8589

Wisconsin
Alphabet Soup
Madison, WI 53705
608-238-1329
Barbara's Yarn Garden
Racine, WI 53402
262-632-7725
Monterey Yarn
Green Bay, WI 54311
920-884-5258

Wyoming
In Sheep's Clothing
Laramie, WY 82070
307-755-9276
Knit on Purl
Jackson, WY 83001
307-733-5648
Over the Moon
Sheridan, WY 82801
307-673-5991
Sheridan, WY 82801
307-673-5991

WEB RESOURCES

The Craft Yarn Council
www.craftyarncouncil.com
The Crochet Guild of America
www.crochet.org

SELECTED SUPPLIERS

www.buy-mail.co.uk
www.coatscrafts.co.uk
www.colourway.co.uk
www.coolwoolz.co.uk
www.designeryarns.uk.com
www.diamondyarns.com
www.ethknits.co.uk
www.e-yarn.com
www.handworksgallery.com
www.hantex.co.uk
www.hook-n-needle.com
www.kangaroo.uk.com
www.karpstyles.ca
www.kgctrading.com
www.knitrowan.com (features worldwide list of stockists of Rowan yarns)
www.knittersdream.com/yarn
www.knittingfever.com
www.knitwellwools.co.uk
www.lacis.com
www.maggiescrochet.com
www.mcadirect.com
www.patternworks.com
www.patonsyarns.com
www.personalthreads.com
www.sakonnetpurls.com
www.shetland-wool-brokers-zetnet.co.uk
www.sirdar.co.uk
www.spiningayarn.com
www.theknittinggarden.com
www.upcountry.co.uk
www.yarncompany.com
www.yarnexpressions.com
www.yarnmarket.com

Index

Credits

Quarto would like to thank the models—Laura Caird, Claire Lithgow, Gillian Cook, and Nikki Goodwin.

All photographs and illustrations are the copyright of Quarto Publishing plc.

AUTHOR'S ACKNOWLEDGMENTS

Many thanks to Kate Buller and all the team at Rowan for their help and support, and for the use of their gorgeous yarns and beads. Thanks also to Irene Jackson and Lavinia Blackwall for helping me create the final projects, and to all my friends, especially Andy for his help and encouragement.